Dance Daughters of the Most High!
Book 2

More Amazing Stories of Long Overlooked and
Underappreciated Women in the Old Testament

Dr. Bill Senyard

ISBN- 979-8-9912476-3-4

All Scripture quotations, unless otherwise stated, are from the Holy Bible: New International Version (NIV). Copyright 1973, 1978, 1984 by International Bible Society.

Cover artwork by Beverly Ash Gilbert.

Contents

Chapter One

Introduction

Welcome to Dance, Daughters of the Most High! Book 2. In the first Dance book, we told the incredible stories of seven often overlooked, primarily unappreciated, or misunderstood mothers of our faith. The feedback has been encouraging. There appears to be a hunger for more stories about the heroic, unknown women of our biblical past.

Much of the inspiration for the Dance came from a recent visit to the Women's Atrium at the Magdala Monastery in Galilee—the purported hometown of Mary Magdalene. It features eight pillars, seven of which represent by name remarkable valued women who followed Jesus: Mary Magdalene (Luke 8:2), Susana and Joanna, the wife of Chuza (Luke 8:3), Mary and her sister Martha (Luke 10:38), Salome, the mother of James and John, Simon Peter's mother-in-law (Matthew 8:15), and Mary, wife of Cleopas (John 19:25). Pillar #8 honors nameless women of faith across all time.

I remember the moment I walked around the expansive hall, reading the women's names on the columns and being surprised and saddened that I knew so little about each one. These were special people, and I didn't know their stories. Few in my group did beyond recognizing their names. I challenged myself to remedy the gap as best as I could. Not being a woman, I have not had to struggle in a culture that has its thumbs on the scales way too often. But I am a storyteller. I hope to render their stories in a way that resonates with modern women.

Imagine an expanded Daughters of the Most High Hall filled with a myriad of #8 Pillars, each recounting the stories of remarkable, little-known women of the Old and New Testaments inspiring this next generation of women—and men. Doesn't that sound like a worthy project? We would have to expand the Women's Atrium or add another floor or two, but it would attract attention all over the globe.

Who were these historically, often neglected, #8 Pillar Daughters of the Most High that are everywhere in the biblical text? In some ways, before God called them, they were much like women today, with ordinary lives littered with regular struggles, disappointments, joys, and relationships. And then God pursued them, embraced them, and filled them with Heaven-born fruit and calling. Any objective person can see they were special.

God still does this today. He interrupts our worlds, converges our story with His, and sweeps us into the mysterious celestial dance imbibed with the potential of great purpose for unlikely heroes and heroines alike.

To be clear, God does not pursue those who are worthy. That is a modern theological misconception. God bestows worth upon the formerly unworthy—male and female equally.

So, how have we so often missed the stories of these women? One reason is we have mainly relegated them to male storytellers. It makes sense. One modern actress lamented about the lack of female directors and writers in movies even today.

> For the most part, I was surprised by the representation of female characters onscreen. I do hope that when we include more female storytellers, we will have more of the women that I recognize in my day-to-day life. (Jessica Chastain)

As I embark on this project, I am aware of the potential danger of that in this volume. I am not a female storyteller, but I am a storyteller. I will do my best to present these women in a way that is recognizable and real. I plan to enthusiastically retell the stories of these women accurately, interestingly, and in a way that resonates with girls and women today. As a male, it is a great privilege to undertake this task. These women deserve it.

In the first Dance book, we looked at God's plan for honoring the childless Hannah, the underestimated Ya'el, and the unnamed mother of Samson. God's treatment of each was in massive contrast to the women's lot during the toxically misogynistic period of the Judges. We looked at Zipporah, the black woman who stood up to God Himself. There was the unnamed wise woman who singlehandedly saved an entire city from one of David's psychopathic generals. Lastly, we heard the story of Princess Jehosheba, who, at great personal risk, rescued David's line. Her story reads like a Jack Ryan novel.

The women we will examine in this book also span all three major periods of the Old Testament—two from the time of the Patriarchs (Rebekah and Tamar), two from the period of the Exodus (Shiphrah, Puah), and three from the age of the Kings (Abigail, Widow of Zarephath, Huldah). Our last daughter of the Most High transcended all ages or times (the Shulamite). At least two of the eight weren't even Jews.

I am committed to telling their stories afresh. First, because the voices of these daughters of the Most High should be heard by all men and women today, and second, to give testimony of what God's Spirit does, particularly in the lives of those the world has often treated disproportionately. God enveloped these women with great honor beyond their expectations. God's historic valuing of women speaks volumes to us today.

Important Note: The Critical Role of the Holy Spirit

In the Old Testament period, the work of God's Spirit was not always as obvious as in the New Testament. Yet there were times when the biblical author notes that the Spirit temporarily came upon this or that person to do something beyond their normal capacity and experience (i.e., Joshua-Numbers 27:18; Othniel-Judges 3:10; Gideon-Judges 6:34; Jephthah-Judges 11:29). I am suggesting that even though the Spirit of God is not explicitly mentioned in the case of these daughters of the Most High, I am satisfied that we can see tangible evidence of the Spirit's working—His fingerprints, His DNA, and His heart for others. Here are five manifestations of the Spirit of God.

Uncommon Sensitivity to God

These daughters of the Most High seemed especially aware of what God wanted them to do and were empowered with a tremendous compulsion to obey, even at significant risk. Simply put, they seemed to hear God's voice when no one else around them did.

At great risk, Rebekah chose to become Isaac's wife, leaving her home and family to traipse into the great unknown with a man she had not even met.

The prophetess Huldah was asked to determine whether a discovered scroll was actually the word of God—the Bible. Humanly speaking, who in the world would be qualified to do that? You couldn't just Google 'scroll' or ask ChatGPT, "Is this divinely inspired writ?" We think the scroll was what we call the book of Deuteronomy today. But back then, it was just a lone, dusty scroll discovered in temple construction debris. What a head trip for any prophet, but even more so for a woman prophet in the patriarchal world of the late 7th century BCE. Huldah seemed to hear God's voice clearly.

Supernatural Wisdom

Wisdom is highly valued in our world even today. Some people come to mind: Mother Theresa, Einstein, DaVinci, Martin Luther King, Rosa Parks, and Plato—so many more. We may disagree with some of them, but few would argue against their shrewdness.

God-sourced wisdom is similar in many ways, yet also wildly different. Some of these daughters of the Most High tapped into profound wisdom beyond their context. In particular, they seemed to be supernaturally aware of the ongoing, often invisible conflict between God and His enemies, the latter who sought to destroy God's people. God's wisdom, it seems, is less interested in personal gain and glory and much more interested in rescuing and saving His people. God's wisdom typically answers, "How can these helpless people be rescued?"

These wise daughters of the Most High manifested remarkable wisdom, diplomacy, and rhetorical skills that ushered God's peace and resolution (i.e., shalom) into very contentious situations—at times without a shot fired.

As uncomfortable as this might be to modern Christians, these wise women would sometimes need to use disinformation, obfuscation, and even flat-out lies to protect the vulnerable people of God. From God's point of view, there are times in the conflict with the enemy when the right strategy calls for misinformation. It is a war, and the potential costs are high. These ideal women with God-sourced wisdom got it. I will say more, but there is a place for subterfuge in war.

For instance, the lowly Hebrew midwives, Shiphrah and Puah, seemed empowered with God-smarts. They outsmarted the great Pharoah of Egypt and almost single-handedly prevented a complete genocide of God's people. They are unsung heroes.

Righteousness

Don't be scared off by this theological word. It's true, we don't use it much day-to-day. And unfortunately, many modern Christians use it largely incorrectly. "Righteousness," they say, "is about doing right and obeying the law." Very confusing.

Using righteous synonyms, like selfless, hospitable, sacrificial, and other-oriented is much better. Righteous women and men in the Bible were those who thought of the well-being of others over themselves. They overflowed with hospitality and were willing to sacrifice comfort to honor and care for others. This righteousness was in Jesus' DNA and was manifested perfectly on the Cross, where he suffered and died for the sake of unrighteous, unworthy others.

The pagan widow of Zarephath seemed to have such selflessness—even Jesus would say so. She gave her last bit of food to honor a total stranger, someone who wasn't from her tribe, even though it would likely lead to the death of her son. That was sacrificial hospitality.

In our account of Abigail, we will see a stark contrast between her and her dolt of a husband, the unrighteous Nabal ('fool'). He cared little for anyone other than himself and his reputation. In contrast, she was willing to act righteously and stave off an ugly slaughter that would have politically damaged King David's reputation.

Dependence Upon God

This is a difficult concept to grasp today. We in the West have been taught explicitly or implicitly that our highest goal is independence, self-sufficiency, and individualism.

Today, dependence is a four-letter word and is consigned to the same categories as slavery, surrender, brokenness, and the like. In fact, many Christian women have been bludgeoned by a bat labeled by dependence's evil stepsister, 'submission.'

But dependence upon God is a very different thing. It is a positive fruit of the Spirit, an intentional and free reliance upon the capacity of the loving Creator. These daughters were willing to give up their illusions of control and follow God, giving of themselves freely for vulnerable others. This type of dependence carries no negative element of subordination, slavery, or subjugation. It does not mean being right or wrong or doing right or not doing wrong: no grades, no judgment, no shaming, no weakness.

Instead, it is an act of choice by an honorable free agent empowered by the Spirit. Such submission is not in us, humanly speaking, no matter how hard we try. It must be accessed.

News flash! God created humans to be dependent upon His Spirit, not independent. Independence is one of Satan's characteristics that got him in trouble. The same was true for Jonah, the sons-in-law of Lot, Adam and Eve, Judas, Nabal, Jacob, and many people throughout Israel's history.

It is important to acknowledge that even these daughters of the Most High struggled with dependence. We all do. Dependence was very difficult for the Shulammite in the last chapter of this book. Her past experiences of submitting to love only to be hurt, shamed, and used had left deep scars. How could her shredded, traumatized midbrain ever allow her to depend again? You'll see. Her story is good news for women and men today.

Assurance of God's Favor

Child psychologist Urie Bronfenbrenner said, "Every child needs at least one adult who is irrationally crazy about him or her." Amen.

Some of these daughters of the Most High seemed to 'get' that they were walking in such favor with God Himself. The Spirit empowered them to begin to grasp the limitless love of God for them as they were, not as they should be or could be (cf. Eph. 3:14-21).

It is as if they could hear God whispering in their ears, "You are my beloved daughter, with whom I am well pleased."

Can you imagine the difference that makes?

This fruit of the Spirit is such good news for modern women and girls who feel diminished, overlooked, and dismissed by culture—those who feel a little like second-class citizens.

To be clear, I am suggesting these women were cut out of the same cloth as women today. They weren't born with an awareness of the favor of God nor a sacrificial desire to serve others selflessly. God found them as they were, in their particular contexts, and sent them on a quest for great glory and name. He embraced them, filled them with His Spirit, and invited them into the celestial dance. These women chose to enter that dance not because someone with power demanded it of them but because they wanted to. They deserve a #8 Pillar in the expanded Hall of Daughters of the Most High.

Be encouraged, women. God is actively inviting women today to dance the same dance.

Jireh

The worship song, Jireh by Maverick City and Elevation Worship, brilliantly communicates what I am talking about. The name of God, "Jireh" (Hebrew: Yir'eh- literally means 'to make you see'), comes from the difficult story of Abraham and Isaac in Genesis 22. God commanded Abraham to do something inconceivable. He was to sacrifice his only son, Isaac. Can you imagine? How could he do that? Why would he do that? I suggest God endowed him with supernatural sensitivity, wisdom, dependence, and assurance of favor.

Empowered by God's Spirit, like the Daughters of the Most High in this book, Abraham achieved something far beyond his capabilities. Honestly, none of the heroic women we will explore were innately capable, strong, or wise enough, humanly speaking, to accomplish their God-given quest.

That's where God's name, 'Yir'eh,' comes in. At the very last moment, as Abraham raised his sharp, bone-cutting knife in the air, Isaac bound by ropes upon the crude altar, God made Abraham "see"—yir'eh—a ram caught in a thicket.

You can almost hear God saying, "See Abraham, I have provided your sacrifice, a substitute for your only son, Isaac, whom I also love. I am enough for you and Isaac. Look, I even made you see it."

We get the significance. In the end, God provided His only Son on the Cross to be the substitutionary sacrifice for all my sins. And like with Abraham, God miraculously made me see it. He was my Yir'eh. I was never enough to fix my countless legal issues against the Heavenly throne. He was always enough.

> So, Abraham called that place The LORD Will Provide (Yir'eh).
> And to this day it is said, "On the mountain of the LORD it will
> be provided (Yir'eh)" (Gen 22:14).

In the song, they do a brilliant thing. Most translate Jireh (yir'eh) as "God provides." They translate it as "the Lord is enough." I love it. They have brilliantly captured the core of the ancient word.

Enoughness is a big deal in our culture. Enoughness is related to our present experience of value and worth in our own eyes and our perception of how others see us—men and women alike. Here is David Zahl in Seculosity:

> Listen carefully and you'll hear [the] word "enough" everywhere, especially when it comes to the anxiety, loneliness, exhaustion, and division that plague our moment to such tragic proportions. You'll hear about people scrambling to be successful enough, happy enough, thin enough, wealthy enough, influential enough, desired enough, charitable enough, woke enough, good enough. We believe instinctively that, were we to reach some benchmark in our minds, then value, vindication, and love would be ours. [1]

It is related to shame. Shame happens when I realize I am not experiencing enoughness and believe it is my fault somehow. Something is wrong with me. Something is broken, something is off. I am not enough to have a real relationship where someone gets me and likes me, where my life matters to others and to God. We jones for enoughness. But honestly, it is difficult to attain in these cold, hard, and selfish streets of planet Earth.

Here's the beautiful, so-often well-kept secret. We can begin to feel enoughness when we stop striving to earn it and instead hold empty hands skyward to receive yir'eh from God. When we experience this fullness of God (Eph 3:14-21), we won't need to garner enoughness from other sources, many of which have dangerous consequences.

God was enough in Genesis 22 and is still enough. Even if he had offered his son, Abraham's sacrifice would not have been enough. His son wasn't a sufficient sacrifice to cover anyone's sins. He wasn't enough. But God is enough.

None of the women whose stories we will tell in this book were enough either. God made them see that He was yir'eh for them. He is the same for you and me today. Please stop reading now and Google Jireh; sit back, watch, and listen. Do the long play and drink it in. Here are some of the lyrics.[2]

I'll never be more loved than I am right now.

Wasn't holding You up,

So there's nothing I can do to let You down,

It doesn't take a trophy to make You proud,

I'll never be more loved than I am right now.

Going through a storm but I won't go down

I hear Your voice,

Carried in the rhythm of the wind to call me out.

You would cross an ocean so I wouldn't drown.

You've never been closer than You are right now.

You are Jireh, You are enough

Jireh, You are enough

And I will be content in every circumstance

You are Jireh, You are enough.

Forever enough, Always enough

More than enough, Forever enough

Always enough, More than enough

I'm already loved, I'm already chosen

I know who I am, I know what You've spoken

I'm already loved, More than I could imagine

And that is enough.

Again, no shaming, not here. No guilt trip to manipulate or leverage you to work harder. We are not giving you three steps to become more "good enough." (Sorry for the bad grammar.) We start by saying none of us are enough. Same for men and women alike. You will not be enough even if you are more righteous, faithful, considerate, sacrificial, feminine, or masculine. Yet, God is enough with you as you are. He is Yir'eh. Your part in the relationship? Ask to experience His yir'eh.

Once again, these traits look equally good on men. Christ had them all.

Important Reminder!

Whether or not you access this fruit of the Spirit today, tomorrow, or the next day, it does not change how much God adores you. Christian, Jesus loves you perfectly right now. He can't love you anymore or any less than he does right now. He loves you far more than you love—or don't love– yourself. You cannot improve on this love or take away from it.

But if your heart desires to experience more of the benefits of what Christ purchased for you, we will show you how. You can do this—just not on your own.

As you ask God to give you His power through the Spirit of Christ in your inner being (Eph 3:14-21), you will begin to experience even more of the five fruit of the Spirit on your own God-ordained quest. Say this gospel presentation aloud, beloved of the Most High. I invite you to speak it aloud to your nasty, critical inner voice at least twice daily.

> Jesus-Follower, daughter of the Most-High, strictly because of what Jesus did for you 2000 years ago, Jesus loves you with all His heart, as much as the Father loves the Son and the Son loves the Father. God loves you as you are, not as you should be or could be. You can't add to this love or take away from it. It often feels like you've messed it up or need to do something so God will like you better. Not so. How do you experience it more? Simple! Ask the Spirit inside you to make you know, experience, and feel just how much God loves you right now. Just ask. Ask again later today. Ask tomorrow. Make it a spiritual habit.

Then, dance, daughter of the Most-High, dance (Eph 3:14-21).[3]
Welcome to Dance, Daughters of the Most High! Book 2.

Engage Questions:

1. What did you learn that you did not know before? What difference does it make to you in your world today?

2. Consider the five fingerprints of the Holy Spirit working in people's lives, then and today. Did one of them resonate with you in particular? Explain.

3. What struck you when you heard the Simple Uncluttered Gospel? Was there a single word or phrase that jumped off the page? Did something bother you? Do you agree with the Simple Uncluttered Gospel? Please share any thoughts.

---

1. Zahl, "Seculosity," 109-126.

2. Moore, "Jireh."

3. You can get Women's Simple Uncluttered Gospel bookmarks at https://gospel-app.com.

Chapter Two

The Fool's Wife

In the late Midrash, Abigail is listed among the twenty-three truly upright and righteous women who came forth from Israel.[1] It is a great honor.

I can only imagine her unfortunate marriage. "Will you, Abigail, 'My Father God is Joy,' lovely in form like the matriarch Rachael and intelligent, take this arrogant, unperceptive, selfish, lout of a man, whose well-deserved nickname, Nabal, meaning 'fool,' to be your wedded husband?"

It rolls off the tongue, doesn't it? It sounds more like something out of Monty Python. One can't think of a more unlikely couple. In those days, families generally arranged marriages. My guess is Abigail's parents were thrilled to betroth their daughter to this extremely wealthy businessman.

I am not judging. Hopefully, Abigail's parents desired love for her as well. Marrying a successful businessman who owned 3000 sheep and a thousand goats who roamed the pastures and hills just south of Hebron assured her of comfort and reputation for the rest of her life—and the dowry wasn't anything to be frowned upon, I would guess.

It is not likely his name was actually Nabal. One wonders if the scribe wanted the reader to know that this man was referred to as the 'fool'—likely behind his back.

Is this story just unfortunate, or is there a parallel related to our heavenly marriage with Jesus? "God, my father-joy" is clumsily wed to 'fool.' Something to ponder in all humility. To me, it sounds like God's sense of humor.

Here's where the story begins. It was spring, and the time for sheep shearing celebrations was at hand. David's band of 600 highly trained men were in exile, still hiding from King Saul. But in the meantime, they earned their living by offering uncontracted protection for the sheepherders who flourished south of Hebron.

Some modern Christians are uncomfortable with David's effort. It feels like he was running a protection racket, something from the Godfather.

In ancient times, such protection would have been welcomed and quite valuable. Think of it as an extension of the traditions related to hospitality.

Today, a businessperson would hire guards or soldiers to protect their assets. In those days, herdsmen, particularly those with the wealth of Nabal, would rely on mercenaries like David and gladly share the bounty with them during the spring shearing season. It was how things worked.

Offering kindness and bounty to neighbors who were in alliance with you was not only reasonable but also considerate of the future. If you offended the guards and they removed themselves, your business would experience significant losses the following year.

The bottom line is that it was culturally and economically the right thing to do. Not doing it would be foolish (a nabal) and a huge offense, comparable to shaming. And let's face it. What fool would do anything to shame a highly trained army of 600 soldiers? Oh, that's right. Nabal, the fool, would.

The story might have been different if David had been muscling in, but he had done nothing. One of Nabal's men testified to Abigail that David's men had earned hospitality.

> *Yet the men were very good to us, and we suffered no harm, and we did not miss anything when we were in the fields, as long as we went with them. They were a wall to us both by night and by day, all the while we were with them keeping the sheep. Now therefore know this and consider what you should do, for harm*

*is determined against our master and against all his house,
and he is such a worthless man that one cannot speak to him.
(1 Sam 25:15-17)*

So, David sent a small delegation to Nabal with a greeting and a reasonable request. Shockingly, Nabal acted like an idiot.

*But one of the young men told Abigail, Nabal's wife, "Behold,
David sent messengers out of the wilderness to greet our master,
and he railed at them" (1 Sam 25:14).*

He "railed" at them (Hebrew: 'its). The word has the connotation of the shrill sound that a bird might make. He screamed at the envoys, belittled them, and dressed them down. In no world would this have been smart or appropriate. Nabal had a very low EQ and would suffer consequences for how he treated allies. Per one site,

> Low emotional intelligence (low EQ) refers to the inability
> to accurately perceive emotions (in both yourself and others)
> and to use that information to guide your thinking and
> actions. You may know someone who never seems to be
> able to control their emotions or understand the feelings
> of others. Perhaps they are constantly doing or saying the
> wrong things, at the wrong time. Or maybe they're always
> judging others, but have a hard time accepting criticism. If
> this describes someone you know, chances are high that this
> person struggles with low emotional intelligence.[2]

In other words, a fool.

Now enters our female hero, Abigail. In the first Dance book, the wise woman of Abel-Beth-Maacha stood up on the tottering parapet and bid Joab, the general, to come to her and hold an official audience. Abigail also prepared for her official audience with David.

Men are often caricatured as shooting from the hip, erupting in immediate reactionary behaviors, and saying things in the heat of the moment that they may regret later. They often do this because they seem willing to end up in a fight where one person wins and another loses. Having said this, I also know women who would fit this description.

More often, women seem to take a wiser approach: set the stage, choose the right words, establish an overarching tone, and aim for shalom, where the two sides don't fight but rather live in peace. It is not a perfect peace, not this side of heaven; it is generally better than the more testosterone endpoint. Having said this, I know of men who would also fit this description—just fewer of them.

Abigail was a wise woman. She prepared a bountiful audience gift for David who was angry and on the way to destroy Nabal. It's not exactly a parallel, but I see the situation in Defcon One. DEFCON, short for Defense Readiness Condition or simply Defense Condition, is the U.S. military's ranking system for defense readiness for a potential nuclear attack. Defcon One means destruction is imminent unless something remarkable happens.

In this situation, the remarkable thing that defused Defcon One was a person. We can presume this was more than David and his men would have ever expected.

> *Then Abigail made haste and took two hundred loaves and two skins of wine and five sheep already prepared and five seahs of parched grain and a hundred clusters of raisins and two hundred cakes of figs, and laid them on donkeys. And she said to her young men, "Go on before me; behold, I come after you." But she did not tell her husband Nabal. And as she rode on the donkey and came down under cover of the mountain, behold, David and his men came down toward her, and she met them. (1 Sam 25:18-20)*

We can see Nabal's shortsightedness. Abigail ended up offering to David only five of Nabal's 3000 sheep. It's a no-brainer. Abigail clearly did the right thing in the right shalom-building way.

The official audience was now established and indirectly agreed upon by both parties. Abigail had provided an audience gift suitable for a king to an angry, offended David. She at least had his attention—downshift from Defcon One to Defcon Two. For a moment, David's wounded finger was off the red button.

Again, referencing the first Dance book, you might remember the story of the wise woman of Abel-Beth-Maachah. At this point in her détente, she said to Joab, "Behold, your handmaid." It was a show of public humility and respect. It cost her little and removed one more barrier to the negotiation for the survival of her entire family and city.

Abigail went even further.

When Abigail saw David, she hurried and got down from the donkey and fell before David on her face and bowed to the ground (1Sam 25:23).

Nothing in her actions could have been misunderstood or misconstrued by even the most testosterone-riddled male on the planet—downshift to Defcon Three, where the forces remain in a readiness response mode, waiting for further orders. Matters could escalate to Defcon One in a heartbeat. Things were still tense.

The wise and beautiful Abigail had to walk a very fine line. She would try to validate David's injustices but, simultaneously, not express disloyalty to her husband, fool or not. For kings, loyalty was sacrosanct. If she came across as self-serving or a disloyal wife, David might dismiss her as a foolish woman, a nabal-wife.

Abigail did something remarkable, which I suggest is incomparable in all Scripture. It has been noted that she mentions the Lord's name seven times in eight verses. The tone of the negotiations had shifted from what's right and wrong, who's right and who is wrong, what injustices had occurred, and what must be done in revenge to subtly reminding David of the spiritual dimensions of his God-calling. He was not just any warlord offering protection to sheep. He was the future King of Israel, the "son of God." He was to rely on the wisdom that comes from God and leads to shalom for God's people.

The next thing she did was most remarkable. Without justifying her husband's selfish and evil actions, she asked David to put Nabal's rightful punishment upon her.

> *She fell at his feet and said, "On me alone, my lord, be the guilt. Please let your servant speak in your ears, and hear the words of your servant. Let not my lord regard this worthless fellow, Nabal, for as his name is, so is he. Nabal is his name, and folly is with him" (1 Sam 25:24-25).*

She had brilliantly threaded the needle. She demonstrated an understanding of David's sense of injustice and anger, loyalty to her husband, willingness to be his redemption price, and cemented herself as an ambassador worthy of being heard.

The tension in the place dropped from an ancient equivalent of Defcon One to Defcon Four, where forces are looking for more intelligence to inform their next move. For the moment, the slaughter of Nabal and his men was no longer imminent but still on the table as an option.

Let the détente continue at the skilled, adept hand of "My Father is Joy."

She now requested that David accept the gift from her hand as reparation for the former offense.

It's a win-win. David's honor was restored, his men were rewarded, and there was no bloodshed that might bring God's anger upon the house of David. (1 Sam 25:25b-27).

She continued with a rapid-fire succession of God's name and eloquent blessing. Please forgive the trespass, and certainly God will bless you.

> *Please forgive the trespass of your servant. For the LORD will certainly make my lord a sure house because my lord is fighting*

the battles of the LORD, and evil shall not be found in you so long as you live. If men rise up to pursue you and to seek your life, the life of my lord shall be bound in the bundle of the living in the care of the LORD your God. And the lives of your enemies he shall sling out as from the hollow of a sling. And when the LORD has done to my lord according to all the good that he has spoken concerning you and has appointed you prince over Israel, my lord shall have no cause of grief or pangs of conscience for having shed blood without cause or for my lord working salvation himself. And when the LORD has dealt well with my lord, then remember your servant. (1 Sam 25:28-31)

You may know the rest of the story. David withdrew from the expected slaughter, and a tenuous peace was ushered in. All by the wisdom and rhetorical skills of a single, undoubtedly Spirit-empowered daughter of the Most High.

Briefly, when Abigail told Nabal what happened, he had a heart attack and died. Eventually, she became David's second wife—sounds a bit like a made-for-TV movie.

Speaking of made-for-TV, may I suggest the perfect Israeli actress to play the shrewd and beautiful Abigail? The actress would need to be able to express a vulnerable yet smart compassion on the one hand but have the street smarts required to reach just compromises when and where necessary. The beautiful Odelya Halevi is a Yemenite Jew born in Israel. She is best known for her complicated role as ADA Samantha Maroun in *Law & Order*. Look her up. She would rock the part of the intelligent, loyal, and compassionate Abigail. If you could get Lior Raz to play the stubborn and angry Nabal, we could be looking at Best Picture awards. He usually plays heroes, but this would be a wonderful stretch for him. What do you think?

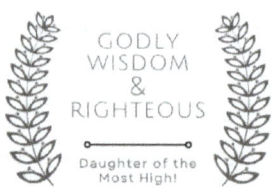

Abigail deserves an honored #8 Pillar in the Hallowed Hall of the Daughters of the Most High. On the column should be a banner recognizing that she manifested the spiritual fruit of wisdom and righteousness. Do you agree? Can you identify any of the other spiritual attributes?

Engage Questions:

1. What did you learn that you did not know before? What difference does it make to you in your world today?

2. How would you describe what Abigail did in your own words? Have you done something similar? Or do you know someone who has?

3. What do you think God was doing behind the scenes? How does this narrative speak to the role of girls and women in society today?

4. What are your thoughts on Odelya Halevi and Lior Raz playing Abigail and Nabal? What's your take on this casting? (You know I'm right here, don't you?)

---

1. Kadari, "Abigail"; Maller, "Abigail."

2. Cherry, "Low Emotional Intelligence."

DANCE
DAUGHTERS
OF THE
MOST HIGH!

Chapter Three

Pharoah's Match

Have you ever had to choose between your faith and orders from your employers, spouse, government officials, or laws? It is a dangerous place to be, and often, there are consequences for not obeying, even if you know what they are asking of you is wrong.

You would not be the first. Things in this groaning world are rarely black and white. Sometimes, hearing the clarity of God's voice in the din is difficult. So, we must lean into faith, whatever that means to you. It can be frightening, but there are times that women (and men) of faith, those for whom Jesus paid the price of corporal punishment, must disobey instructions from those other voices.

We will look at perhaps the very first biblical example of civil disobedience in the name of faith. These early women stood alone against the greatest dictator of the greatest superpower of their day. And who were they? Two enslaved women.

The new Pharoah had a problem. It was complicated. He inherited it from the previous Pharaoh, and in his mind, it potentially threatened the integrity of the great empire of Egypt.

The chronicles told the story. A Hebrew named Joseph—a high-level government official—though a foreigner, brought great wealth to Egypt during an extended famine. But he also had relocated seventy of his tribe to Egypt. They "multiplied greatly and became exceedingly numerous so that the land was filled with them" (Ex 1:5-7). Who would have guessed that they were this fertile?

In the leader's mind, the Hebrews were on a population trajectory that would eclipse the number of Egyptians in Egypt. Exaggeration? Paranoia? Antisemitism? Racism? Tribalism? It's hard to say; it's likely all the above.

He came up with a vile plan. He first tried enslaving the Jews, putting them into harsh labor camps, denigrating them as sub-Egyptians. But God thwarted this dehumanizing strategy and multiplied the Hebrews even more (Ex 1:11-12).

Like the Romans after them, the Egyptian leadership and elite worried about a massive slave revolt that would take down the empire. So, Pharoah instituted the Evil-Genius Plan B. If all the Hebrew boys were systematically murdered by the Hebrew midwives at birth, a forced genocide by their own hand, the rate of increase in the Hebrew population would be shattered in a single generation. The girls would grow up and marry into Egyptian families. The Hebrew race, the descendants of Abraham, the firstborn of Yahweh, would disappear from the world in 30, maybe 40 years.

It was a diabolical plan and appeared unstoppable until two mere Hebrew slave midwives, Shiphrah and Puah, stood up against the regime at great personal risk to themselves and their families.

The king of Egypt said to the Hebrew midwives, whose names were Shiphrah and Puah, "When you help the Hebrew women in childbirth and observe them on the delivery stool, if it is a boy, kill him; but if it is a girl, let her live." The midwives, however, feared God and did not do what the king of Egypt had told them to do; they let the boys live. Then the king of Egypt summoned the midwives and asked them, "Why have you done this? Why have you let the boys live?" The midwives answered Pharaoh, "Hebrew women are not like Egyptian women; they are vigorous and give birth before the midwives arrive." So, God was kind to the midwives and the people increased and became even more numerous. And because the midwives feared God, he gave them families of their own. (Ex 1:15-21)

On a higher celestial stage, or maybe better the heavenly chess board, if Satan could manipulate the powers that be to destroy all of Eve's promised seed, he would win. But the master chess player, Yahweh, would use two daughters of the Most High, mere slaves at the very bottom of the societal power pyramid, to crush the head of the serpent again (Gen 3:15)—a massive shaming for the arrogant deceiver.

These two Hebrew slaves would thwart the plans of the mighty Pharoah. Unlike Moses after them, they seem implacable, brave, and loaded with chutzpah and shrewdness. You want them on your side.

I believe Shiphrah and Puah embody at least three of the five attributes of the ideal biblical woman. I am curious what you think.

- An Uncommon Sensitivity to God

- Supernatural Wisdom

- Righteousness

An Uncommon Sensitivity to God

We know very little about them, but their names are interesting. Shiphrah means 'fair one,' which was likely given to a lovely baby by proud parents. Puah was probably a Canaanite word for "little girl." Perhaps a smaller-than-normal infant, but the name stuck.

So, in this corner, the feared king of the greatest superpower on the planet, reigning heavyweight champion, undefeated in 100 bouts, Pharoah the Magnificent. In the other corner, two challengers, their first bout of any kind, each 5 feet 4 inches and weighing in at 120 pounds each—wet, Fair One and Little Girl. It was wonderfully comical. Vegas would likely not even give 1000 to 1 odds—too lopsided for anyone to take that bet.

But we are let in on a little secret that so often tilts the balance of power to favor the most unlikely. Think David versus Goliath. Think Gideon versus the Midianites. Think Paul versus Rome.

These two women 'feared the Lord.' I like how one source put it. "The Torah has no word for religion. The closest related concept found in the Torah is 'the fear of God.'[1]

Don't think Stephen King or Freddie Kreuger terror. The 'fear of the Lord' is a syntagm. Per Oxford reference, "a syntagm is an orderly combination of interacting signifiers which forms a meaningful whole." In plain English, while the words carry a specific meaning individually, they take on a whole new connotation when you wed them together. To fear the Lord is to intentionally follow him in faith, to prioritize His will over yours, and to submit to his priorities, although it disadvantages you and may cost you dearly.

So, as I studied this, I wondered what the Hebrew religion looked like then. The Hebrews had been out of the promised land for over 400 years, that's thirteen generations. Had they lost the early Abrahamic enthusiasm for God? If you go to Ancestry.com and try to discern much about your great, great, great, great, great, great, great, great, great, great, great grandfather's religion, how granular would the report be? It gets even worse; they were slaves for perhaps 150 years, five generations. By the time of the Exodus, I wonder if they were more Egyptians than Jews.

Would the Egyptian taskmasters even have allowed them to worship their ancestor's God? Is it reasonable for the memories of Abraham, Isaac, and Jacob to have devolved a little or a lot?

Do we have anything that would point us to this conclusion? Here's something.

During that long period, the king of Egypt died. The Israelites groaned in their slavery and cried out, and their cry for help because of their slavery went up to God (Ex 2:23)

I grant it is inconclusive, but the text says they just cried out. When this occurs, there is most often an object to their cries. They would cry out 'to God.' But there is a gap here, an omission. Is it telling?

Here's an equivalent. If you are in trouble, take out your smartphone and dial any number again and again, and eventually, the police somehow get wind of your need and respond. How much did you actually trust in the police if you weren't trying to dial 911?

I can't be sure, but it does raise the question.

There was also the first meeting between Moses and the Hebrew elders and leaders.

> *Moses and Aaron brought together all the elders of the Israelites, and Aaron told them everything the LORD had said to Moses. He also performed the signs before the people, and they believed. And when they heard that the LORD was concerned about them and had seen their misery, they bowed down and worshiped. (Ex 4:29-31)*

Whatever they thought about the Lord before Moses' story, they were convinced of the existence of such a God after he did the miraculous signs. When Moses testified this God of miraculous parlor tricks also cared about them, they bowed and worshipped. I am assuming that the nature of their worship before this was somehow different, if there was any at all. I wouldn't be surprised if Yahweh had simply become one of the vast pantheon of Egyptian deities.

I am sure the two Hebrew midwives somehow had a dynamic relationship with the God of Abraham, Isaac, and Jacob. Whether they were part of a minority remnant or not, Moses referred to them as fearing the Lord. This entailed identifying with Yahweh as their God and desiring to obey Him and His prescripts, but it also included a trust that He was a God who indeed cared for them and His people of covenant, His firstborn.

True faith in Yahweh somehow survived the generations in Egypt, in the hearts and minds of at least two women. This is an excellent example of "an uncommon sensitivity to God" that marks the best of the best of the daughters of the Most High.

Give me two women of such faith, and you can change the world; you can compete with great evil, you can take down oppressive empires, end racism, sexism, economic disparities, and challenge poverty, slavery, and genocide. In God's hands, these are those who will accomplish what he designs.

Righteousness

Next, these two women were willing to prioritize the well-being of others over their own, i.e., righteousness. While we see such sacrificial love in humans here and there, it is part of God's core DNA. God is other-oriented by nature. Check out Psalm 113.

> *The LORD is exalted over all the nations,*
> *His glory above the heavens.*
> *Who is like the LORD our God,*
> *The One who sits enthroned on high,*
> *who stoops down to look*
> *on the heavens and the earth?*
> *He raises the poor from the dust*
> *And lifts the needy from the ash heap;*
> *He seats them with princes,*
> *With the princes of their people.*
> *He settles the barren woman in her home*
> *As a happy mother of children.*
> *Praise the LORD. (Psalm 113:4-9)*

We candy-coat this in English. Though God rightly is on the throne of all the heavens, he stoops down, humiliating Himself (humanly speaking), not for his own sake but to glorify the poor and needy. This is His DNA, the DNA of Jesus, and the Holy Spirit in our inner being (Eph 3). This is the essence of righteousness.

Paul says the same thing about Jesus in Philippians 2:

> *Do nothing out of selfish ambition or vain conceit, but in humility consider others better than yourselves. Each of you should look not only to your own interests, but also to the interests of others. Your attitude should be the same as of Christ Jesus: Who, being in very nature God, did not consider equality with God something to be grasped, but made himself nothing, taking the very nature of a servant, being made in human likeness. And being found in appearance as a man, he humbled himself and became obedient to death-- even death on a cross! Therefore, God exalted him to the highest place and gave him the name that is above every name, that at the name of Jesus every knee should bow, in heaven and on earth and under the earth, and every tongue confess that Jesus Christ is Lord, to the glory of God the Father. (Phil 2:3-11)*

This is the nature of God the Father, Jesus, and the Holy Spirit in our inner being. What does it look like? It resembles the reflection of glory in the faces of 'Fair One' and 'Little Girl.'

Not only did they fear God, but they also looked a lot like Him. After all, the larger context of the Exodus was God coming to redeem his firstborn son, Israel. We know that it would eventually cost Him His own Son.

Supernatural Wisdom

That leads us to a beautiful, instructive twist in the story of these two intrepid heroes of Judaism. You might first shudder at what I am about to tell you, but don't shoot the messenger. The third characteristic of Spirit-filled Daughters of the Most High is that sometimes, to defeat the enemies of God and his people, they act very shrewdly—to the point where many would be bothered.

In this case, the two women justified blatant disobedience and lying to Pharoah.

> *Then the king of Egypt summoned the midwives and asked them,*
> *"Why have you done this? Why have you let the boys live?"*
> *The midwives answered Pharaoh, "Hebrew women are not like*
> *Egyptian women; they are vigorous and give birth before the*
> *midwives arrive" (Ex 1:18-19).*

They prevaricated, slipped one past, pulled the wool over, hornswoggled, lied like a rug, passed on alternative facts, pinky swore, and even dissembled the truth.

Yes, I know what you are thinking. Thou shalt not lie. Am I right? Technically, those words are not written yet, not for another 80 years, but that does not help us much. Neither Shiphrah nor Puah was ever criticized or condemned by God or anyone else, for that matter. As their account was compiled and edited, likely during or after the Exile, the scribes, concerned about honoring the Torah, could have scrubbed the story somehow. They d idn't.

What do we make of this? Is the moral of the passage that you can disobey authority and lie anytime you want? Nope.

Rules have contexts. The wise person who fears the Lord must consider the situation. A modern example of an exception to breaking laws about deception is baseball. You can and are even encouraged to steal a base in the game. In football, you can make someone believe you are going one way and then go another. There is a popular game called Liar, Liar. Here are the instructions.

> Gameplay: Players tell a truth or a lie in each round, depending
> on their assigned role. Players score points when other players
> incorrectly identify their truth as a lie—or their lie as a truth.
> There's always a liar!

Can Christians play Liar, Liar? Of course, they can. Lying is part of the game.

These are lighthearted examples, but in the case of Shiphrah and Puah, they were battling evil. To God, this was not a game; it was the fulfillment of His promise to His people.

So, while it is a sin to lie against your spouse, your boss, or others, it is kosher to lie in some instances to defeat the enemies of God, those who seek to harm His people.

This takes wisdom, of course. It also takes a sensitivity to the Spirit in our inner being. It takes humility because 100% clarity is rare.

Shiphrah and Puah were great Jewesses, examples of those who risked their lives for the sake of others, and their successful strategy was to lie to those in power. There may come a time, when your God-ordained quest will put you in a situation where, to save the lives of God's people, or guard the faith, or stem the tide of evil strongholds in this groaning creation, you may need to lie, misrepresent, stretch the truth, obfuscate, muddy the waters—and you may be punished for your actions.

In their case, Little Girl and Fair One pulled it off and stayed a massive genocide of helpless Hebrew babies. God protected them and blessed them.

So, God was kind to the midwives and the people increased and became even more numerous. And because the midwives feared God, he gave them families of their own (Ex 1:20-21).

It is not entirely clear what the Hebrew meaning of 'he gave them families of their own' is, but it describes a good thing.

Women of faith, you are invited to be filled with the spiritual DNA of God and go and act accordingly. It is a high honor to stand up against destructive powers. Deborah did it. Paul did it. Samson, Gideon, Elijah, Esther, Abraham, Jael, and the most outstanding example would be Jesus; all did it. Eve didn't, nor did Adam.

There are times, daughters of the Most High, when it is not wise or godly to submit to authorities over you. You must use shrewdness to honor God and save lives. A clear example is in the case of a physically abusive spouse. You may be called to assist in a rescue using deceit and shrewdness to protect the victimized partner.

There are times to challenge church authorities. It could cost you. There are times to challenge entire governments. Spirit-filled wisdom is necessary to be sure.

There are times, daughters of Eve, to defeat God's enemies, you must consider "godly deceit" as an option. This requires God-sourced wisdom from living in fear of the Lord, or in New Testament lingo, being filled with the Spirit.

Who could take on the movie role of one of these great, understated women, Puah and Shiphrah? Irit Kaplan is a well-known actress in Israel on both stage and screen. She is best known for her role as the dour matriarch Merceda Ermoza in the Netflix hit series *The Beauty Queen of Jerusalem*. She is such a formidable character that one wonders if Pharaoh would even have a chance.

So, follow me. If we wanted to bring some comedic relief to Kaplan in this wonderful account, we could cast Maya Rudolph along with her? Maya is Jewish on her father's side. She told The New York Times that she says her family is "agnostic Jewish because my grandfather didn't like being told what to do." That is the chip on the shoulder these characters might need.

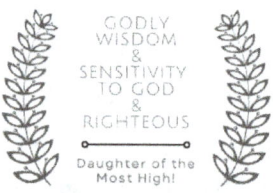

These two, Shiphrah and Puah, received glory as co-saviors of God's people. In so doing, we remember them as true mothers of life ('Eves'). They deserve a #8 Pillar in the Hallowed Hall of the Daughters of the Most High. On their column should be a banner recognizing the fingerprints of the Spirit of God in at least three attributes: an uncommon sensitivity to God, supernatural wisdom, and Heaven-born righteousness. What do you think? Do you see evidence of any other fruit?

Engage Questions:

1. What did you learn that you did not know before? What difference does it make to you in your world today?

2. What do you think about what we said about 'godly deceit?' This is a safe place. There is clearly room for dialogue.

3. The author said, "Give me two women of such faith, and you can change the world; you can compete with great evil, you can take down oppressive empires, end racism, sexism, economic disparities, and challenge poverty, slavery, and genocide. In God's hands, these are those who will accomplish what he designs." How does that hit you? Could you be another one of these women of faith?

---

1. Shiphrah and Puah, Wikipedia.

DANCE
DAUGHTERS
OF THE
MOST HIGH!

Chapter Four

Jesus' Sermon Illustration

O nly twice did Jesus use women from the Old Testament as sermon illustrations of what faith and righteousness should look like. In both cases, the women were not even Jews. Both deserve a #8 Pillar in the Hallowed Hall of the Daughters of the Most High.

The Queen of the South

Jesus was engaged in a particularly heated confrontation with some Pharisees and other teachers of the law. They demanded he demonstrate who he was by tossing down a few miraculous signs—which he had already done on several occasions.

Note: miraculous signs never saved or convinced anyone of Jesus' deity. Jesus would have none of it.

> *A wicked and adulterous generation asks for a miraculous sign!*
> *But none will be given it except the sign of the prophet Jonah. For*
> *as Jonah was three days and three nights in the belly of a huge fish,*
> *so the Son of Man will be three days and three nights in the heart of*
> *the earth. The men of Nineveh will stand up at the judgment with*

this generation and condemn it; for they repented at the preaching of Jonah, and now one greater than Jonah is here. (Matt 12:38-40)

Here is the essence of what he was saying.

Can't you blind men see? The tens of thousands of pagan unbelievers in Ninevah—of all places—fell to their knees in faith and repentance at the revelation of the very faulty human prophet Jonah. But you, supposedly faithful God-worshipping religious men are not only unmoved by the preaching of someone far greater than Jonah—you even challenge the prophet, showing no deference at all to the word of God—no sensitivity to God. (Remember the fingerprints of the Spirit?) God favored the repentant Assyrians more than you who claim Abraham's DNA and yet will not bow and worship God who is standing in front of you.

Jesus was not finished. After he threw the faith of an entire Assyrian city (a country historically hated by the Jews) into their shocked, full-bearded faces, he further shamed them with the remarkable story of the Queen of Sheba.

The Queen of the South will rise at the judgment with this generation and condemn it; for she came from the ends of the earth to listen to Solomon's wisdom, and now one greater than Solomon is here (Matt 12:38-42).

This unbelieving non-Jewish woman showed more deference and interest in the God-given wisdom of Solomon than these religious men did to God's wisdom-incarnate, Jesus. Even worse, she traveled an extreme distance from Ethiopia at great expense and risk to hear wisdom from Solomon. Ironically, not so the Pharisees, Solomon's distant relatives. Jesus traveled the extreme distance at significant risk instead of them. The contrast is stark.

Unlike this woman who showed what I suggest was heaven-born sensitivity to the voice of God, these religious, institutional men would prefer parlor tricks to God's wisdom revealed. Shameful. It's embarrassing, really—though I wonder, if I were there, would I have joined them in this mockery of the wisdom of God?

These men were as needy for a real relationship with God as the people of Ninevah and the Queen of Sheba. But they were not open to being rescued and receiving God's love. Their rejection of God's love was not just a missed opportunity, it was a cause for regret and sorrow, just as it is for us today.

Be encouraged! Jesus noticed and publicly proclaimed the faith of this unnamed foreign woman.

The Widow of Zarephath

Another Old Testament woman Jesus referenced in a sermon illustration was an unnamed gentile widow from a country that was also no friend of Israel. Jesus held her up as an example of true sensitivity to the voice of God and an exemplar of Proverbs 31 righteousness. Like the Queen of Sheba, she was likely not a Jew either.

You probably remember the account. It was at the beginning of Jesus' ministry. He had already been baptized by John and endured suffering and temptation at the hand of Satan in the wilderness. His ministry was expanding; people were beginning to listen and to follow—until he came to his hometown of Nazareth. Here is Luke's account of what happened there.

> *Jesus returned to Galilee in the power of the Spirit, and news about him spread through the whole countryside. He taught in their synagogues, and everyone praised him. He went to Nazareth, where he had been brought up, and on the Sabbath day he went into the synagogue, as was his custom. And he stood up to read. The scroll of the prophet Isaiah was handed to him. Unrolling it, he found the place where it is written: "The Spirit of the Lord is on me, because he has anointed me to preach good news to the poor.*

He has sent me to proclaim freedom for the prisoners and recovery of sight for the blind, to release the oppressed, to proclaim the year of the Lord's favor." Then he rolled up the scroll, gave it back to the attendant and sat down. The eyes of everyone in the synagogue were fastened on him, and he began by saying to them, "Today this scripture is fulfilled in your hearing." (Luke 4:16-21)

At first, the response from family and neighbors to his message seemed positive. But Jesus knew better—he was God, after all. He knew His message had found no root in his hometown.

All spoke well of him and were amazed at the gracious words that came from his lips. "Isn't this Joseph's son?" they asked. Jesus said to them, "Surely you will quote this proverb to me: 'Physician, heal yourself! Do here in your hometown what we have heard that you did in Capernaum.'" "I tell you the truth," he continued, "no prophet is accepted in his hometown. I assure you that there were many widows in Israel in Elijah's time, when the sky was shut for three and a half years and there was a severe famine throughout the land. Yet Elijah was not sent to any of them, but to a widow in Zarephath in the region of Sidon. And there were many in Israel with leprosy in the time of Elisha the prophet, yet not one of them was cleansed — only Naaman the Syrian." All the people in the synagogue were furious when they heard this. They got up, drove him out of the town, and took him to the brow of the hill on which the town was built, in order to throw him down the cliff. But he walked right through the crowd and went on his way. Then he went down to Capernaum, a town in Galilee, and on the Sabbath began to teach the people. They were amazed at his teaching, because his message had authority. (Luke 4:22-32)

A little context. It's funny how history gets rewritten sometimes. In Jesus' Lower Galilee, the region including Nazareth, the great prophet Elijah had become the pride and joy of the Jews. Elijah, though born east of the Jordan River, did the bulk of his preaching and miracles in Galilee, one of the most significant happened only a stone's throw from Nazareth (2 Kings 4). After nine hundred years, the Lower Galileans had, for all practical purposes, adopted Elijah as one of their great heroes of the faith. Think of him as an honorary Galilean.

But the dirty little embarrassing secret was this was not the case. Elijah's Israel was under a harsh curse for her rampant unfaithfulness and her unwillingness to hear and repent of crimes against God. So, God sent a drought to the area that lasted three and a half years. (1Kings 16:30-17:1)

Jesus reminds the Nazarenes that his predecessor, Elijah, also found himself unwelcome in the region. The people had to blame someone, right? So God shockingly sent the great prophet far away to minister to pagans instead.

You can see why this got under the Nazarene leaders' yarmulkes. Jesus was strongly implying—at a religious synagogue in very religious Nazareth—that little had changed in nine centuries. To quote the great baseball player and philosopher Yogi Berra, it was "Déjà vu all over again." Like in Elijah's day, the God of Israel was persona non grata—in Israel. So, he would move on to where people were willing to hear—those more sensitive to his voice. Tragically, Nazareth was no friend to God. Ironically, proving Jesus' very point, the people of Nazareth grew enraged. They attempted to throw God's son off a cliff (Luke 4:29). Prosecution rests.

But according to Jesus, there was one woman who was indeed sensitive to God's voice—not even a believing Jew. Indeed, God's sense of humor. She would have been the most surprised that God, or any god, cared much for her. Her life looked more cursed than blessed. But that is about to change. She was pursued by God and, like all the other women in the hallowed hall of the Daughters of the Most High, was given a glorious quest she had not asked for or imagined. In the end, she was hallowed as a great woman of faith and righteousness—so says Jesus.

Let's pick up the story of Elijah and the Sidonian widow in 1 Kings 17.

Then the word of the LORD came to [Elijah]: "Go at once to Zarephath of Sidon and stay there. I have commanded a widow in that place to supply you with food." So he went to Zarephath. When [Elijah] came to the town gate, a widow was there gathering sticks. He called to her and asked, "Would you bring me a little water in a jar so I may have a drink?" As she was going to get it, he called, "And bring me, please, a piece of bread." "As surely as the LORD your God lives," she replied, "I don't have any bread—only a handful of flour in a jar and a little oil in a jug. I am gathering a few sticks to take home and make a meal for myself and my son, that we may eat it—and die." Elijah said to her, "Don't be afraid. Go home and do as you have said. But first make a small cake of bread for me from what you have and bring it to me, and then make something for yourself and your son. For this is what the LORD, the God of Israel, says: 'The jar of flour will not be used up and the jug of oil will not run dry until the day the LORD gives rain on the land.'" She went away and did as Elijah had told her. So there was food every day for Elijah and for the woman and her family. For the jar of flour was not used up and the jug of oil did not run dry, in keeping with the word of the LORD spoken by Elijah. (1 Kings 17:8-16)

What a great story and a miracle by any measure. It is also a wonderful picture of the inclusivity of the love of God for the unlovable. God pursued and rescued this poor, unbelieving woman who was not of the loins of Abraham. That was what our God did then and still does today.

I would love to meet and chat with this woman in Heaven. If anyone had the right to be cynical, depressed, atheist, or angry, it would be her. Life had thrown her some nasty curveballs. Since her son was still living with her, we could guess that she was likely in her twenties, still relatively young. Her husband was gone, so she made do on her own. We could also assume that her parents were deceased. Otherwise, they might have taken care of her and her son.

Isolated, with no apparent resources to fight against the famine caused by the drought, she prepared to die, she and her son. Can you imagine?

And yet, when this Jewish stranger asked for water and food, she stopped her search for firewood and went to the local well and brought him water. No complaint was recorded, no bargaining or whining. She willingly reached out to serve a stranger in need.

One of the fingerprints of the Spirit working in the hearts and minds of women—and men—is righteousness. In the introduction, I identified this as the motivation for being concerned with the welfare of others over self. This fruit of the Spirit causes the overflow of hospitality and the willingness to sacrifice comfort to honor and care for others. This righteousness was in Jesus' DNA and manifested perfectly on the Cross, where he suffered and died for the sake of unrighteous, unworthy others.

In the case of the widow of Zarephath, God revealed in her a surprising, miraculous generosity that could have cost her and her son's life. She did the righteous thing above and beyond any call of duty, not knowing that Elijah's God would do anything. She was moved to feed the hungry Elijah and her son and then die of starvation.

Is it any wonder later rabbis of the Mishnah acclaimed her, though not a Jew, a powerful example of the Proverbs 31 wife, whom they call the Eshet Hayil, Woman of Valor?[1]

"She opens her arms to the poor and extends her hands to the needy." Quite an honor for a Lebanese pagan woman.

But wait a minute. Undoubtedly, some of you have observed this widow wasn't as righteous as she seemed on the surface. God had to command (tsawah) her to be hospitable to Elijah (1 King 17:9). Why didn't God command someone in Israel and spare Elijah the journey? Surely they would have obeyed, right?

Apparently not. God had already commanded Israel to care for others, particularly the poor and strangers. The greatest of all commandments is to love God and your neighbor over self.

In ancient Israel, hospitality was not merely a question of good manners, but a moral institution which grew out of the harsh desert and nomadic existence led by the people of Israel. The biblical customs of welcoming the weary traveler and receiving the stranger in one's midst was the matrix out of which hospitality and all its tributary aspects developed into a highly esteemed virtue in Jewish tradition. Biblical law specifically sanctified hospitality toward the *ger* ("stranger") who was to be made particularly welcome "for you were strangers in a strange land" (Lev. 19:34 and see Ex. 12:49). The Midrash ... relates that even at the height of Nebuchadnezzar's siege of Jerusalem, mothers would deprive their children of the last crust in order to grant hospitality to a mourner.[2]

But such righteousness and hospitality were nowhere to be found in the Israel of Elijah's day or that of Nazareth in Jesus' day.

A second fingerprint of the Spirit we observe in many remarkable women in the Old Testament—certainly those worthy of a #8 Pillar in the Hall of the Daughters of the Most High is they have a heaven-born uncommon sensitivity to God and his voice. They hear God somehow, despite their circumstances. These special daughters of the Most High seem to be aware of what God wants them to do. God empowers them with an extraordinary compulsion to obey, even at great risk and harm.

This widow was a case in point. When God found her, she had nothing, in fact, only enough flour for a small biscuit—a final meal for her and her only remaining family, her son. But then God...

She was likely pagan, so humanly speaking, as far as we know, she did not know Elijah's God. Even if she knew of such a god, why would she rationally believe he would care one iota about her family's well-being? I imagine her asking, "Where was this God when I needed him before? Why in the world would I trust Him now?"

She had nothing to do with this God before, nor He with her, she would have likely assumed. He owed her no favors, no mercies. And even if this God existed and had such a power and will, why would she reasonably have much confidence in Him? His official representative and ambassador, Elijah, hadn't fared much better than she. He had to flee for his life from God's own people. That would give her little hope or confidence. To top it all off, what kind of compassionate deity would suffer his people with a three-and-a-half-year drought?

Honestly, there were a dozen reasons she would not believe in this new God. And yet, she does—#8 Pillar worthy.

> *She went away and did as Elijah had told her. So there was food every day for Elijah and for the woman and her family. For the jar of flour was not used up and the jug of oil did not run dry, in keeping with the word of the LORD spoken by Elijah (1 Kings 17:15-16).*

The story could end here with great dancing and singing, with an installment of her column in the Hallowed Hall of the Daughters of the Most High. But God was not yet done with this amazing woman and her nascent, fragile faith—not just yet. Left alone, her faith would probably have devolved into the shadowy, fractured version mostly evident in Israel. It seemed God wanted more for this daughter. God continued to blow on the flame in her spirit. Maybe you've experienced something like this as well.

> *Some time later the son of the woman who owned the house became ill. He grew worse and worse, and finally stopped breathing. She said to Elijah, "What do you have against me, man of God? Did you come to remind me of my sin and kill my son?" "Give me your son," Elijah replied. He took him from her arms, carried him to the upper room where he was staying, and laid him on his bed. Then he cried out to the LORD, "O LORD my God, have you brought tragedy also upon this widow I am staying with, by causing her son to die?" Then he stretched himself out on the boy three times and cried to the LORD, "O LORD my God, let this boy's life return to*

> *him!" The LORD heard Elijah's cry, and the boy's life returned*
> *to him, and he lived. Elijah picked up the child and carried him*
> *down from the room into the house. He gave him to his mother*
> *and said, "Look, your son is alive!" Then the woman said to*
> *Elijah, "Now I know that you are a man of God and that the word*
> *of the LORD from your mouth is the truth." (1 Kings 17:17-24)*

We moderns often have a warped and confused understanding of Biblical faith. There are two large categories of faith. The common use of the word faith in our day-to-day lives speaks of confidence in the validity of some matter. For example, I believe it will rain today, or I believe going to church is a good thing.

Common synonyms for this faith are: believe, be convinced, trust, have confidence in, consider true, accept, strongly guess, bet, conclude, give credence to, identify with, set my life's standards to live by, etc.

However, there is a narrower biblical faith that is similar in many ways but of a very different substance and source.

> *But the fruit of the Spirit is love, joy, peace, patience, kindness,*
> *goodness, faithfulness... (Gal 5:22).*

The faithfulness in Galatians 5:22 is the Greek pistis. In common usage, it can be translated faithfulness, but the twenty-plus other times it is used in Galatians, it is translated as faith. This faith is a heaven-sourced fruit of the Spirit, like love, joy, peace, kindness, etc., that is innate to God alone, not of our DNA whatsoever.

This second kind of faith must be given to us by God. We didn't have it before he intervened and manifested it in our hearts and minds. Since it is of God, it should be noticeable.

Think about it: if injected with the love of God, we should feel loved a little or a lot and even love others more. It is the same with faith. As recipients of this heaven-sourced faith, we will feel more confident that God loves us, sees us as his beloved child, and has our back even in troubled times. We might more often hear him saying over us, "You are my beloved son or daughter with whom I am well pleased."

It is not a result of a class, sermon, bible study, or us having done anything. We can ask for it, but the Spirit gives it to us as He wills.

> *All these are the work of one and the same Spirit, and he distributes them to each one, just as he determines (1 Cor 12:11).*

Now, I believe this is what happened to this wonderful woman who had—a little while before—virtually given up. All alone in the universe, she had resigned herself and her son to starvation. She likely had prayed ceaselessly to her deity or deities, with no result. There was no hope, no rescue, and no one had her back for a long time. But then God... Miraculously, she believed—a little or a lot. A powerful new attachment to this God had begun.

But now what? Many Christians wrongly believe this second category of faith is static. You either have faith, or you don't. It doesn't grow; it can't be stretched. It is what it is.

But nothing could be further from the truth. It can grow in the life of a child of God in two ways. The Spirit can give more faith to us (1 Cor 12:11), or God can write, direct, produce, and have a critically important cameo role in a life quest in which our tiny faith is stretched to its limit—where it is challenged often at great sacrifice and pain.

The good news for Christians is since this faith is of the Spirit and the Spirit dwells in our inner being, we can never lose this faith. But God seems to desire that our faith will grow. He is very committed to making it happen.

I am not suggesting this process makes sense to me—or that I like it. This attribute of Godly faith grows under trial and testing and is far above my pay grade. My reasoning remains woefully incapable of explaining how such God-ordained pain, loss, and suffering can lead to a new experience of the love of God for me, but there it is. In such trials, I can viscerally fear God has abandoned me while, at the same time, know God is right beside me and has my back. Have you experienced such a thing?

The Apostle Paul recognizes this working of God in the lives of those he loves.

> *For we do not want you to be unaware, brothers, of the affliction we experienced in Asia. For we were so utterly burdened beyond our strength that we despaired of life itself. Indeed, we felt that we had received the sentence of death. But that was to make us rely not on ourselves but on God who raises the dead (2 Cor. 1:8-9).*

I suggest that through the death of her son, her only son, the widow seemed to have gained a greater experience of her God-given faith. How do we know? She complained to God's prophet, Elijah, evidence of her new, alien faith. She now 'knew,' she says, that the God of Elijah was also her God. This attachment was beyond emotionalism. This was identity level-awareness.

In her badge at the top of this chapter, we ascribed to her two attributes of Spirit-Filled Daughters of the Most High, a sensitivity to the voice of God and a righteousness that desired to put others first. What do you think? Do you see other fingerprints of the Spirit?

Widow of Zarephath: The Movie

Many commented how they enjoyed my foray into casting for the movie versions of our heroine's story. Many Lebanese actresses would be excellent choices. I was struck by the work of Lebanese actress Darina Al Joundi, perhaps best known for the award-winning movie, *Our River...Our Sky* (2021). When playing her part, Darina owns the screen. She would be a very impassioned and believable widow of Zarephath. Check out her bio.

In closing

I want to loop back to Jesus' sermon in Nazareth. He told the people at the synagogue He came to preach good news to the poor, proclaim freedom for the prisoners and recovery of sight for the blind, release the oppressed, and proclaim the year of the Lord's favor.

This was precisely what God did to that poor woman through Elijah. She experienced the favor of a God she didn't know existed and would never have imagined would pursue her. God owed her nothing. And yet He gave her everything. But this is what God does, then and now.

In Zarephath of Sidon, God finds a broken, poor, pagan dying widow who was very special and different from all the women and men of Israel at her time. Though she suffered in the same toxic atmosphere that enveloped the entire Levant, she proved to be an unlikely Daughter of the Most High. She was a brilliant light that shone brightly in that dark place—even nine centuries later. So says Jesus.

She deserves a #8 Pillar in the Hallowed Hall of the Daughters of the Most High.

Engage Questions:

1. What did you learn that you did not know before? What difference does it make to you in your world today?

2. What would it be like to be used as a sermon illustration by Jesus Himself?

3. What does it tell you about the inclusivity of God that so many gentile women are represented honorably in the Hall of the Daughters of the Most High? Try to put it into your own words.

1. Kadari, Widow of Zarephath.

2. Hospitality, Jewish Virtual Library. "Foreign travelers, although not protected by law could count on the custom of hospitality. It was also the duty of the elders of the cities of refuge to succor, as well as to protect, the unwitting killer who sought refuge in their cities until the death of the high priest. Isaiah states that one of the duties of the pious is to "deal thy bread to the hungry," and to "bring the poor that are cast out to thy house". The Bible is replete with examples of pious hospitality (Gen 18, 19, 24, Ex 2:20, Josh 2, 1 Sam 25, Job 31:32, Judges 13:15, 19, 2 Kings 4:8-11)... Breaches of hospitality, on the other hand, were punished (Jud 8:5-9. 19:22, 1 Sam 25)... Rabbinic literature widened the scope of the virtue of hospitality, which it called *hakhnasat orehim* (lit. "bringingin of guests"). It was considered a great mitzvah, an expression of *gemilut hasadim* ("kindness"), especially when it was extended to the poor...Hospitality is...even more important than prayer or ...receiving the divine presence."

Chapter Five

The Maligned Widow

This woman's story is not widely publicized in Christian circles. You certainly don't hear it in children's church or on 'visitation' Sunday. Honestly, it is a bit of an embarrassment to modern Christians. It feels more like modern reality TV than the high bar for behavior we expect in the lives of Biblical characters, especially the Jewish patriarchs.

To make a long story short, Judah slept with his daughter-in-law, the same Judah who was the famous forefather of King David and Jesus. Then, in the understatement of the ages, he declares,

She is more righteous than I (Gen 38:26).

How can we look our teenagers in the eyes and explain this one?

This narrative is a reasonable admission of improper behavior in anyone's book. Granted, there were some extenuating circumstances. Judah did sleep with his daughter-in-law, thinking that she was a temple prostitute. The plot thickens, but not in a good way. This story is worse than reality TV.

And what about the woman, Tamar? What's her story? It turns out she was the mastermind behind the mess. You can't make this up.

Now we see why most modern commentators want to keep the Tamar story at arms or football-field length. And yet, drum roll...Jewish scholars see Tamar in a very different light. To many, she is a hero of the faith.

> Although her behavior could be interpreted as an act of sexual licentiousness and wantonness, the midrashim defend Tamar and praise her. They describe her as a woman with sterling qualities, who maintained the strictures of modesty and faithfully observed the laws of [yibbum] (levirate marriage customs) ... and her behavior shows the proper way in which all future women should perform.[1]

Now are you curious? This is the story of the Canaanite Tamar, the daughter-in-law of Judah, of Jesus's ancestral line. This bizarre tale gives us new insight into the confusing dynamics of power, justice, and agency that women struggled with during the patriarchal period in Judea. But can we honor her with a #8 Pillar in the hallowed Hall of the Daughters of the Most High? We will see.

Let's set the context. Judah and his brothers had just sold Joseph into slavery. Judah was fourth in line for the Abrahamic birthright, meaning he had almost zero expectations he would ever be the future tribal patriarch upon his father's death. To his credit, he does have some misgivings about the horrible crime against Joseph (Gen 37:26-27), but not enough to stop his brothers.

We will see this indifference and cowardice to do what was right as a pattern in Judah's life. Remember, we defined righteousness as that God-born motivation to look after the well-being of others, even if at great risk to ourselves. Judah did not manifest such righteousness during the Joseph narrative.

Judah was also out of sync with the family marriage philosophy established by his father and grandfather. Instead of traveling to upper Mesopotamia (Haran/Paddan Aram, see Gen 24 & 29) to find a bride within Abraham's extended family, he chose a local Canaanite woman, a non-Abrahamic outsider, the unnamed daughter of Shua, to be his wife. Later, Rabbinic scholars lament that Judah, in so doing, betrayed the way of his forefathers and even the way of all Israel.[2]

Judah and the daughter of Shua had three sons, Er, Onan, and lastly, Shelah. When Er was of marriageable age, Judah "got a wife" for him, Tamar (Gen 38:6); the strong implication was that Tamar, like her mother-in-law, was also Canaanite.[3] Hold on to that thought. We will come back to it in a moment.

Why was the narrator so keen on who was marrying who and if they had any sons? The important passing on of God's promises to Abraham was at stake. The entire narrative structure of Genesis was defined by the Hebrew word "toledoth" (generations). "Indeed, the toledoth themselves are steps in a lengthy process of 'choosing.' Each subsequent recipient was the next 'messiah' who would carry upon his shoulders the authoritative history of God's work."[4]

There's Abraham,

followed by his firstborn son, Isaac,

followed by his firstborn designate, Jacob, and then...?

These linear generations form the essential narrative storyline of the book. These toledoth were the sole conduit for the distribution of the all-important promises of God to Israel and, ultimately, to the entire world. In Gen 17, God told Abraham,

> *As for me, this is my covenant with you: You will be the father of many nations. No longer will you be called Abram; your name will be Abraham, for I have made you a father of many nations. I will make you very fruitful; I will make nations of you, and kings will come from you (Gen 17:4-6).*

Today, we have a phrase, "Just follow the money." Skilled readers of Genesis say, "follow the birthright." Birthright refers to the right of the firstborn designated to inherit his father's authority. All the sons received some of their father's wealth and property. Still, the firstborn received a double portion (i.e., "blessing") and became the in situ leader of the family and heir to the promises God made to Abraham (i.e., "birthright").

What did it look like on the ground? In the case of Jacob's twelve sons, Reuben, the oldest, would be expected to get the "double portion" of inheritance, receive the all-important birthright, and become the unquestioned leader of the tribe, the patriarch, heir to the promises of God. He would dutifully pass the birthright on to his firstborn son, and so on.

The other eleven would divide the rest of the inheritance equally among them. For every $1000 of inheritance, Reuben, the new patriarch, would receive $153.80, and the others, $76.90 each. Not too shabby.

But wait. Reuben didn't get the birthright; Judah did. We know David was of the tribe of Judah, and so was Jesus the Messiah. What's up?

A few cultural and legal caveats are at play that sometimes throw a wrench into the works and make for fascinating reading. First, if any sons died before the "reading of the will" and had no heirs, their portion was divided among the surviving heirs. Or if any had done something to shame the family, they also might be excluded by fiat of the patriarch.

The plot thickens, particularly in this case.

Confused? Trust me. All of this is important to understand Tamar's predicament.

Spoiler alert. To everyone's surprise—certainly denying Jacob any Father of the Year award—Father Jacob passed over the first three sons (Reuben, Simeon, and Levi) and gave the birthright and double portion to son #4, Judah.[5] Here's Jacob's deathbed decision that rocked the entire tribe.

> *Judah, your brothers will praise you; your hand will be on the neck of your enemies; your father's sons will bow down to you. You are a lion's cub, O Judah; you return from the prey, my son. Like a lion, he crouches and lies down, like a lioness—who dares to rouse him? The scepter will not depart from Judah, nor the ruler's staff*

from between his feet, until he comes to whom it belongs, and the
obedience of the nations is his. (Gen 17:8-10)

Modern translation. "Judah, the keys to my favorite jacked-up Ford 150 are yours and all my earthly possessions. Don't mess it up."

Ironically, the proclamation "your father's sons will bow down to you" was one of the things that got Joseph sold into slavery.[6] I love the irony.

Tamar

We can now begin to unpack the Tamar story. Tamar's first husband, also Judah's firstborn, Er, was struck down by God for his "wickedness" before any children were born to them. That leaves Tamar a widow and in a complex and challenging situation.

Don't miss this because it drives the rest of the story. Today, we find it difficult understanding this ancient, accepted custom. But here we go. As a widow, she had a choice. She could wipe her hands of Judah and his family and move on, marry someone else from her tribe. Or she could still honor her marital commitment to the deceased Er, even though he was not a prize of a husband and enter the cultural process of leviratic marriage (yibbum)—not for her sake, but for the sake of Er's legacy. [7]

In a yibbum, the brother of a man who died without children was permitted and encouraged to marry the latter's widow and father a child for his brother's legacy. He was not required to do so. If the brother or the widow refused to participate in the yibbum, it was DOA. In that case, they still had to go through a public renunciation ceremony known as halizah.

What about the laws around adultery? The laws against one sleeping with a brother's wife were superseded in this narrow situation (Lev 18-20). Here's how the later Torah defined it.

If brothers are living together and one of them dies without a
son, his widow must not marry outside the family. Her husband's
brother shall take her and marry her and fulfill the duty of a

brother-in-law to her. The first son she bears shall carry on the name of the dead brother so that his name will not be blotted out from Israel. However, if a man does not want to marry his brother's wife, she shall go to the elders at the town gate and say, "My husband's brother refuses to carry on his brother's name in Israel. He will not fulfill the duty of a brother-in-law to me." Then the elders of his town shall summon him and talk to him. If he persists in saying, "I do not want to marry her," his brother's widow shall go up to him in the presence of the elders, take off one of his sandals, spit in his face and say, "This is what is done to the man who will not build up his brother's family line." That man's line shall be known in Israel as The Family of the Unsandaled. (Dt 25:5-10)

But even in Judah's day, four hundred years before the Torah, leviratic marriages were accepted within various cultures swirling within the region. Remember, Tamar was Canaanite. She very likely was familiar with the practice and her possible choices.

Per accepted leviratic customs, Judah gave Tamar to his second son, Onan, who was to act as levir, a surrogate for his dead brother. Together, they would 'beget' a son to continue Er's lineage.

Like most modern soap operas, things became complicated. It turned out Onan was not so happy about the situation.

But Onan knew that the offspring would not be his; so whenever he lay with his brother's wife, he spilled his semen on the ground to keep from producing offspring for his brother (Gen 38:9).

What was Onan thinking? Remember the earlier discussion of firstborn rights? With Er gone and childless, Onan was technically the firstborn heir apparent of a sizable estate—likely two-thirds (66%) of Judah's sheep and goat conglomerate, plus the birthright.

On the other hand, if Onan did the culturally 'right thing' and honored his deceased brother with a son through Tamar, he would lose up to 62% of his portfolio and the birthright. All of that would pass on to Er's son.

Ouch, that would leave a mark.

Unrighteous Onan made a cold, bottom-line calculation.

I believe if we weren't sure before, we should be thinking by this point in this ugly tale God seemed to want the Abrahamic birthright to pass through Er. If I am right, then Onan was out of sync with God, not Tamar. She seemed to be in sync with God on this matter, even when no one else seemed to agree. Remember, we said some of these special daughters of the Most High seem to be supernaturally sensitive to the voice of God, the will of God on some matter, and they manifested a compulsion to obey, even if the path was outrageous or dangerous.

I should also point out Onan could have refused the union at the beginning through halizah, but that might have upset his father. Instead, he compounded his "wicked" actions by marrying Tamar yet refused to do righteousness for his deceased brother Er.

To that degree, Onan was a reflection of his father. Arguably, he was a passive-aggressive people-pleaser, insensitive to the well-being of others, and unwilling to sacrifice to do the righteous thing. As one comedian said, the tree didn't grow far from the apple.

For one reason or another, God was far from happy with Onan.

What [Onan] did was wicked in the LORD's sight; so he put him to death also (Gen 38:10).

Let's do the math. Only one possible son remained who could honor Er's legacy and do what was right in God's eyes.

At this point, I should cut Judah a little slack—not a lot. Although we know God killed two of Judah's sons for "wickedness," Judah does not. What does Judah do? He was never the heroically righteous type in the first place (remember the Joseph narrative). He got cold feet.

Judah then said to his daughter-in-law Tamar, "Live as a widow in your father's house until my son Shelah grows up." For he thought, "He may die too, just like his brothers." So Tamar went to live in her father's house (Gen 38:11).

There are two schools of thought here. One says Judah was terrified he only had one heir left. So, out of fear or superstition, he hesitated to give Tamar to Shelah. Perhaps she's an ancient twist on the "widow-maker" story. So, Judah made up a face-saving excuse about Shelah being too young to get married, but it appeared he had no plan to "do the right thing."

The second school of thought is that Judah was trying to "do the right thing." After all, he had already arranged for one levirate marriage for Tamar and planned to repeat the process with Shelah when he was of age. He was still too young.

You decide. I get it. Either way, Judah was in a tough situation. Some later Jewish scholars suggest God was punishing him for Joseph-gate and for marrying a gentile wife.[8]

For the time being, Judah sent Tamar back to her father to remain a widow and remain chaste on the pain of death.

Tamar appears to be the victim here. Though she tried to do the righteous thing, she was twice widowed, had no children, and was returned to her father's house. In addition to grieving the loss of two husbands, I suspect Tamar felt great shame, isolation, frustration, and abandonment and was in limbo with little recourse, culturally or legally. Still, she obeyed and dutifully waited. She seemed to remain single-minded in her desire to fulfill her commitment to her first deceased husband, Er.

Months passed. No change. Tamar silently bided her time, growing older and less marriageable each day, waiting for word that Judah would finally give her to be married to Shelah as he implicitly promised.

Tamar found herself trapped in the "system" and its strangling constraints, particularly for women. Though she had been a faithful woman and wife, she was stuck, through the negligence of others, in a murky legal limbo with no representation and no respite on the horizon. No one had her back. No one was coming to her aid.

Conventional avenues of legal respite had been shut down. British jurist William Blackstone is reported to have said, "It is a settled and invariable principle in the laws of England, that every right when withheld must have a remedy, and every injury its proper redress."

This did not seem to be the case for Tamar. What happens when that "proper redress" was unjustly withheld from you, no matter the reason? Perhaps you could go to the local Canaanite judge for redress, but what authority would they have over the Tribe of Jacob?

And what might the charge be? For women during that time to have any hope of justice, they must make a compelling case of abuse. At best, Tamar could claim a "breach of duty" against Judah. But that was a long shot.

The entire trajectory of Tamar's life was in jeopardy. Her livelihood and reputation as a righteous woman hung in the balance, totally dependent upon the actions of her wild card, less-than-heroic father-in-law, Judah.

We understand something far more significant was at stake. God's promises to Abraham a few generations before were also in peril.

Will Tamar accept her unfair lot or pursue respite on her own through unconventional means? What would you do, that is, if you were in that culture and believed that your calling was to give your deceased husband a child by having sex with your brother-in-law? Okay, never mind, that's just crazy from our perspective.

Back to Tamar. That's where her head was, and she was tired of waiting. Tamar grabbed the bull by the horns and did something that seemed rash from our modern perspective. I like this quote from Prof. Rabbi Pamela Barmash,[9]

> Tamar has no power in her society, and "her men" have failed her. Thus, to attain justice, she must use whatever power she has, which, in this case, is the power to seduce.

Let me remind you once again. Technically, according to the custom of levirate marriages, Judah had already declared Tamar a widow so she could choose to remarry into another family. It would have been the easy thing to do, for sure. But not to this righteous woman. In her brain, the "right and godly thing to do" was to do whatever it took to give her first deceased husband a child. She would stubbornly try, even if it destroyed her name and reputation.

So, you are beginning to see where I stand on Tamar's worthiness to be honored with a #8 Pillar. Out of a God-sourced inner love for others over self, Tamar seemed motivated to "do the right thing" for her deceased husband and for Judah's family no matter what it cost her. Sacrificial righteousness is one of the tell-tale pieces of evidence of the Spirit in our lives. She, a Canaanite woman, appeared to be the only one who was hell-bent on doing the right thing, all for the sake of a deceased man.

If she had only thought of herself and her long-term security, I imagine she would have pursued betrothal to another family. Her father could find her another suitable husband. But this stubborn, righteous woman seemed obsessed with doing the right thing even though her strategy was going to rock a lot of boats.

After a long time Judah's wife, the daughter of Shua, died. When Judah had recovered from his grief, he went up to Timnah, to the men who were shearing his sheep, and his friend Hirah the Adullamite went with him. When Tamar was told, "Your father-in-law is on his way to Timnah to shear his sheep," she took off her widow's clothes, covered herself with a veil to disguise herself, and then sat down at the entrance to Enaim, which is on the road to Timnah. For she saw that, though Shelah had now grown up, she had not been given to him as his wife. When Judah saw her, he thought she was a prostitute, for she had covered her face. Not realizing that she was his daughter-in-law, he went over to her by the roadside and said, "Come now, let me sleep with you." "And what will you give me to sleep with you?" she asked. "I'll send you a young goat from my flock," he said. "Will you give me something as a pledge until you send it?" she asked. He said, "What pledge should I give you?" "Your seal and its cord, and the staff in your

hand," she answered. So he gave them to her and slept with her,
and she became pregnant by him. After she left, she took off her
veil and put on her widow's clothes again. (Gen 38:12-19)

She did what? Are you kidding me? This story wouldn't look good on a flannel graph during children's church. Am I right? The parents would write the church a nasty email.

A couple of observations. It is easy to condemn Tamar. But should we?

First, Tamar was not planning incest. The Torah was clear that a father-in-law was not to sleep with his daughter-in-law (Lev 18:15), yet in-law incest rules were suspended for the levirate. The levirate was, after all, only a surrogate for the dead husband and his legacy. Therefore, it was not legally incest in this situation.

Though she could have—and maybe should have—discussed it with her father-in-law first, she was on firm ground legally and culturally. The accepted rules of leviratic marriage allow the father to be a possible surrogate to assure his son a legacy.

Hittite laws around the same period, also known as the Code of the Nesilim, confirmed this option for widows. The code said that 'there is no offense' if a man has a wife and the man dies, his brother shall take his widow as a wife. (If the brother dies, his father shall take her.)[10]

One way or another, Judah and Tamar did not appear to be on the same page. I am guessing she thought her father-in-law would never have agreed.

Second, hypocrisy abounds within the account. It seemed everyone knew Judah would find himself in the tent of a prostitute during the sheep-shearing celebration. No one seemed willing to condemn him for his actions. In contrast, we are often very quick to condemn Tamar as a whore,[11] or at least we like to hold her at a religious safe distance. Just saying.

Her bizarre biblical plan worked like a charm. She became pregnant. Just so we are clear, by means provided in the accepted custom of leviracy, she was impregnated with Er's 'seed' from Judah's loins.

When Judah came to deliver his payment (a young goat) to the unknown prostitute, he couldn't find her.

But later, when Tamar turned up pregnant (v. 24), Judah publicly condemned Tamar to death for being an unfaithful adulteress.

> *About three months later Judah was told, "Your daughter-in-law Tamar is guilty of prostitution, and as a result she is now pregnant." Judah said, "Bring her out and have her burned to death!" (Gen 38:24).*

Could he do this? It would seem so. Legally, Judah was the pater familias and, as the so-called "injured party," unaware he was a participant in the affair, sought redress on behalf of his family's reputation. Irony abounds.

Sidebar: Ancient Prostitution

Prostitution in ancient Israel is a highly debated topic due to the limited historical sources and varying interpretations of religious texts. What we can say is that there were regular street prostitutes and those associated with religious temples. The Bible refers to the former as zonah, female, and kalev as male.[12]

It's essential to understand the cultural context in which Tamar lived. In ancient Israel, social and economic factors often pushed vulnerable women, such as widows, those who had lost their virginity before betrothal, or those without family support, towards survival strategies like prostitution. The practice of prostitution in the ancient Near East, pre-Torah, seemed to have been under no moral censure whatsoever and was likely very common.[13] Might Tamar, or women like her, consider prostitution to survive? Likely so.

There seemed to be at least three categories of sacred temple prostitution. There were professionals, ironically called "holy ones," male (qadesh) and female (qadeshah), who were owned by the deity's temple.

A peculiar feature of the Mesopotamian and Canaanite culture was ritual prostitution. To the temple of the goddesses of fertility (Inanna, Ishtar, Astarte) were attached bordellos served by consecrated women who represented the goddess, the female principle of fertility...The existence of sacred prostitutes shows that the individual worshipers receive in this way communion with the divine principle of life and a renewal of their vital forces.[14]

But there is also evidence of regular women performing sex acts once in a lifetime (pre-marriage) to honor some goddess, or only during certain annual pagan rituals.[15] The historian Herodotus says there was a Babylonian practice (remember this is Abraham's home) that every unmarried woman must offer herself and her body to the fertility goddess at one point. She must voluntarily submit to Aphrodite by having sex with a stranger in the shadows of the sanctuary. The money she received for her service was sacred and given to the goddess. Only after she was discharged from her service could she go home and marry.[16]

Yes, there were even times when, shockingly, the Jerusalem temple employed ritual prostitutes.[17]

Four hundred years after Abraham, the Torah widely condemned the practice of both categories of prostitution.

> *No Israelite man (qadesh) or woman (qadeshah) is to become a shrine prostitute. You must not bring the earnings of a female prostitute (zonah) or of a male prostitute (kalev) into the house of the LORD your God to pay any vow, because the LORD your God detests them (to'evah) both (Dt 23:17-18).*

They are called an abomination (to'evah) to the Lord in the same category as gold and silver from divine images (Dt 7:26), the consumption of meat from unclean animals (Dt 14:3), the sacrifice of imperfect animals (17:1), the wearing of clothing of the opposite sex 22:5), dishonest measures (25:16), secret images of deities 27:15), and the sacrifice of children (12:31).[18]

Finale

As Tamar was led off to be burned alive, this capable lady revealed that Judah was the father.

> *As she was being brought out, she sent a message to her father-in-law. "I am pregnant by the man who owns these," she said. And she added, "See if you recognize whose seal and cord and staff these are." Judah recognized them and said, "She is more righteous than I, since I wouldn't give her to my son Shelah." And he did not sleep with her again. (Gen 38:25-26)*

"She is righteous, more than me," was Judah's prophetic utterance that she was innocent of any sin or abomination. Shamed Judah finally came to agree it was Tamar's cultural right to be given to another family member to bear a child for her deceased husband, Er. Judah seemed to have lost sight of the right thing to do. As we have seen, this was his MO.

Tamar, her father-in-law said, was "righteous." Her singular loyalty to Er, her stubborn ability to find ways to succeed despite the deck being stacked against her, and her willingness to use unconventional approaches secured her place in Judah's posterity and Israel's history. She became the maternal ancestor of David, the great King of Israel, and even Jesus the Messiah.

To those of you who still wonder if Tamar was just a conniving, power-grabbing woman who wanted Judah's inheritance and was willing to do anything, including sex, to achieve her goal, I think it might help to contrast her with Jacob. Jacob used deception to gain the birthright for himself. What he did was selfish, despicable, and without concern for the well-being of others. Biblically, he was the poster child for unrighteousness at that point in his life.

Some have rightly observed that there is a parallel between Tamar's story and one of her well-known descendants, Boaz.[19] If you know the story, Ruth was also a righteous, heroic Gentile widow. Her remarkable story was likewise resolved by levirate marriage.

In Tamar's story, only one person, a non-Jewish woman, seemed to be in sync with God. How do we know? God judged both Er and Onan for not fathering a child with Tamar. It is reasonable to conclude that He wanted to further the line of Abraham through Er. Judah began doing the right thing but petered out. Tamar did what she did not for her own benefit, but to honor her dead husband and his legacy (Gen 38:7). She could have easily remarried elsewhere and lived happily ever after. She was well within her rights to do so without any shame or social stigma. It would have been the easy path.

Instead, she embraced the cost of being honorable and did everything she could do to fulfill her responsibility to her dead husband, even though the risks were very high. She took the hard path because she believed it was right. In contrast to Jacob, she was a poster child for biblical righteousness.

We can get hung up on the uncomfortable practice of levirate marriages. They seem creepy to us. Yet, in those days, and in that culture, for a man to perish without an heir, was a societal tragedy. Levirate marriages were the appropriate way to provide a posthumous legacy.

Tamar gave birth to twins, Perez and Zerah (Gen 38:29-30, 1 Chr 2:4), thus restoring Judah's two lost sons. Ultimately, the birthright will go to Er's leviratic son, Perez, not Shelah. Perez was in the lineage of David and, of course, the Messiah.

Children's author Lisa Tawn Bergen wrote the popular book for toddlers, God Gave Us Two, about what to tell a firstborn when child #2 is on the way. Great book. Here's what a reviewer wrote,

Gently and lovingly, Mama and Papa [polar bear] assure their firstborn that the new baby is a gift from God they want very much, just as Little Cub was—and still is. "God gave us you. Now he's given us two!"

If Bergen were to write a child's book on righteous Tamar's journey, it might sound like this.

> Gently and lovingly, Grandpa finally did the right thing, even though he was tricked into doing it. And you, Perez, are the special miraculous birthright from God. "God gave Er you. In fact, God gave Er two."

Hmmm, it might not be a best seller. What do you think?

I would love to hear your thoughts. The levirate practice is strange for moderns to embrace. Our first reaction is that it is just another form of adultery or promiscuity. But it was nothing of the sort. In that cultural context, God blessed the practice of levirate marriage. Even the Torah approved of it. To put it succinctly, the practice in that day and time was as kosher as unleavened bread.

Believe me, I am not starting a movement to resurrect the practice of such surrogacy to its former Biblical place. I would also say the same thing about the practice of having multiple spouses. May God forbid. It is way out there in today's world.

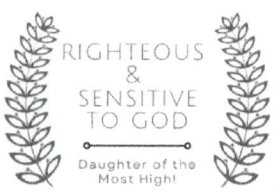

However, Tamar has my vote for a #8 Pillar in the Great Hall of the Daughters of the Most High. But what badge should adorn Tamar's column? I have already mentioned two fruit of the Spirit: a sensitivity and willingness to obey the voice of God and the determination to do right by others even if it could cost you dearly. Time and again, God uses such women, as women, to accomplish His ends even though they are disadvantaged within patriarchal cultures.

Tamar: The Movie

This story would light up the big screen. Maybe Angel Productions could capture the vision, embrace the unorthodoxy, and yet be very sensitive to potential audience discomfort. The title writes itself, Tamar.

I spent some time 'auditioning' Israeli actresses who might pull off the complex role of Tamar. The actress must be relatively young, resolute, capable, and bold. She must also be a bit rebellious while at the same time loyal to a fault.

A few years ago, I watched a powerful short miniseries, *Unorthodox*, starring the Israeli breakout actress Shira Haas (b. Tel Aviv, 1995). It is based upon a true story about an orthodox teenager, Esty Shapiro, whose family compelled her into an arranged Hasidic marriage. She was miserable and could not bear it any longer. She only wanted to find her voice and study music at a Berlin Conservatory. One commentator wrote,

> Etsy is very stubborn but also very flexible. She wants to fit in, but she wants to break out. She is strong, but she is soft. You have to bring this complexity not only to every scene but to every sentence. So this was very attractive to me. I found it amazing, this combination.

Haas played a character like Tamar, who struggled with what she felt was an unjust custom, deep soul-breaking isolation, and little channel for justice or redress. Finally, to survive, she had to take matters into her own hands, even though it cost her dearly.

For your information, Haas was cast to play the superhero, Sabra, in Marvel's latest film, *Captain America: Brave New World.*

Hopefully, she can work on this new project with her busy schedule.

In Closing

Who should resonate and be inspired by Tamar's actions? Are you trapped in a conundrum; two paths lie before you. The first path is a safe bet and easy out. You could take that path and feel no shame or condemnation from anyone.

But down deep in your psyche and spirit, you are convinced that your other choice is the right one, even though you won't benefit at all, and the risk is sky high. You would do this to have someone else's back. You would do this because it is just and right.

Like Tamar, you too may find the powers-that-be are resisting you, putting up roadblocks, or withholding the authority you need to do what you believe is right.

Isolated and powerless, Tamar had to use her intelligence, capability, and even her femininity to accomplish her goal. There was little chance she could overcome the status quo by reacting like a man, so she did what she did as a woman. So impressive.

In my opinion, she deserves to be called a mother of the modern church—and yet, how many churches are named after her? The First Church of Tamar? I am quite sure many out there would disagree.

Engage Questions:

1. What did you learn that you did not know before? What difference does it make to you in your world today?

2. How would you classify Tamar? Was she a truly righteous woman representing ideal biblical womanhood? Or do you still have misgivings? Please explain. This is a safe place. There is room for dialogue.

3. We are learning that God's righteous Kingdom moves through the efforts and lives of very flawed people. Here's a way to think about

it. How many people in this story would you elect as elders in your church? Board members? Deacons? Children's church workers? Isn't that hopeful for us regular, very flawed people? What do you think? Does that trouble you? Go for it.

---

1. Kadari, Tamar.

2. Kadari, Shua's Daughter.

3. Isaac sent his servant to Haran to find a wife from Abraham's extended family. Jacob went to the same region after he fled from Esau and married two relatives. I suspect that if Judah had done the same, the Bible would have noted the similarities.

4. Bull, Toledoth.

5. His older brothers Reuben, Simeon and Levi are passed over by Jacob for a variety of reasons (Gen 17:1-8). Judah becomes the patriarch of the tribe upon Jacob's death. Having said this, at the time of the incident with Tamar, Judah is not expecting the blessing.

6. "[Joseph] said to them, 'Listen to this dream I had: We were binding sheaves of grain out in the field when suddenly my sheaf rose and stood upright, while your sheaves gathered around mine and bowed down to it.' His brothers said to him, 'Do you intend to reign over us? Will you actually rule us?' And they hated him all the more because of his dream and what he had said. Then he had another dream, and he told it to his brothers. 'Listen,' he said, 'I had another dream, and this time the sun and moon and eleven stars were bowing down to me.' When he told his father as well as his brothers, his father rebuked him and said, "'What is this dream you had? Will your mother and I and your brothers actually come and bow down to the ground before you?'" (Gen 37:6-10)

7. Stol, Women. This ancient practice can ensure that the widow has a male provider and protector, of great important in highly patriarchal societies. It also can protect the clan from extinction.

8. Kadari, Shua's Daughter.

9. Barmash, Tamar.

10. Stol, *Women,* 296-299.

11. Twice the narrator refers to Tamar as a *zonah* (Gen 38:15, 24) and twice as a *qadeshah* (Gen 38:20, 21).

12. *Kalev* is most often used pejoratively for feral dogs..

13. Fisher, *Cultic Prostitution.* 225–236.

14. Ibid. 225–236. It should be pointed out that there are some scholars who believe that the notion of sacred sex is a myth or certainly overblown (See, Budin, Sacred Prosstitution).

15. Budin, Sacred Prostitution.

16. Per Herodotus, Histories, "The foulest Babylonian custom is that which compels every woman of the land to sit in the temple of Aphrodite and have intercourse with some stranger once in her life. Many women who are rich and proud and disdain to mingle with the rest, drive to the temple in covered carriages drawn by teams, and stand there with a great retinue of attendants. But most sit down in the sacred plot of Aphrodite, with crowns of cord on their heads; there is a great multitude of women coming and going; passages marked by line run every way through the crowd, by which the men pass and make their choice. Once a woman has taken her place there, she does not go away to her home before some stranger has cast money into her lap and had intercourse with her outside the temple; but while he casts the money, he must say, "I invite you in the name of Mylitta" (that is the Assyrian name for Aphrodite). It does not matter what sum the money is; the woman will never refuse, for that would be a sin, the money being by this act made sacred. So she follows the first man who casts it and rejects no one. After their intercourse, having discharged her sacred duty to the goddess, she goes away to her home; and thereafter there is no bribe however great that will get her. So then the women that are fair and tall are soon free to depart, but the uncomely have long to wait because they cannot fulfill the law; for some of them remain for three years, or four. There is a custom like this in some parts of Cyprus."

17. There were even times that ritual prostitutes plied their wares near the House of Yahweh. The Priest Eli's two sons slept with such women at the entrance to the Tabernacle (1 Sam 2:22). King Josiah ordered the High Priest to tear down quarters in the Jerusalem Temple where male prostitutes (*qadosh*) officially worked (2Ki 23:7). We are told that in 170 BCE, the Seleucid King Antiochus IV Epiphanies, in addition to plundering the Holy temple, he reintroduced sacred prostitutes as part of the Temple worship in spite of the harsh complaints from the helpless Jews. But our story takes place centuries before God gives Moses the tablets of the law, long before God officially condemns the practice in Israel. The "law of the land" in Canaan during the patriarchs? Both ritual and secular prostitutes seemed readily available, both men and women.

18. Post-Torah, prostitutes carried certain social stigmas and their actions and livelihoods were condemned by Torah, the truth of the matter was that they were part of the warp and weave of Israeli and larger Middle Eastern society. When the Israeli spies first entered the land of promise they were saved from being caught by the wiles of a prostitute (*zonah*) named Rahab. Scripture offers no condemnation of her at all. They had equal access to the King's court as any other citizen (1Kings 3:16ff). Neither of these women who brought their legal case before Solomon are condemned for being prostitutes. The Judge Samson partook of prostitutes, and again, Scripture does not seem to condemn him (Judges 16:1). The Book of Hosea uses the metaphor of prostitution to illustrate Israel's unfaithfulness to God. Additionally, the Book of Proverbs warns against being enticed by prostitutes and the dangers associated with such behavior. Prov 7:10ff. gives a scathing criticism to one zonah who is described as having 'crafty intent.' See also (Num 25:1-2, Judges 2:17, 8:27, 33, Jer 3:6, Ezek 6:9, Hos 4:12).

19. Frymer-Kensky, Tamar: Bible.

Chapter Six

The Faces of Rebekah

You probably know her as Rebekah. The etymology of her name is complex. Some suggest the root is found in other Semitic languages and means "to tie fast" or "to secure." Maybe she was a precocious child who wouldn't stop running around and exploring the camp. Perhaps they may have used the equivalent of today's child harness. Others suppose the name suggests her beauty easily ensnared men. Your guess is as good as mine. Today, it is one of the most common names among Jewish families, mainly due to her fame.

Rebekah was born in Haran, a prominent village in Mesopotamia, around 2000 BCE. A little context: this was around the same time the Egyptian Pharaoh Mentuhotep II finally succeeded in unifying Egypt, transforming it into one of two world superpowers. The Babylonians were the other dominant power. They had just conquered the "land between the rivers" and began disseminating Hammurabi's famous code of laws into the culture. They also brought remarkable advances in literature, history, and science. This was Rebekah's home.

Here's an interesting tidbit. Have you ever heard of The Love Song of Shu-Sin? It may be the oldest love song in world history. Some argue it is the template for all love poetry.

Rebekah was likely aware of the song. No doubt, every young unmarried girl would have been familiar with the tune and the lyrics. It topped the music charts for a thousand years. The lyrics are about the courtship and marriage between the shepherd-fertility-god Dumuzi (biblical Tammuz) and his divine spouse, the queen of the gods, the goddess of love, intimacy, and war, Inanna (Akkadian Istar).[1]

For unmarried virgins throughout the empire, likely from any tribe, it spoke of a romantic relationship with a handsome man who would honor and adore her as she was. Interestingly, a millennia later, God will incarnate the crude husks of these poems to present His courtship, marriage, and consummation of love with Israel in the Song of Songs.

It begins with a young man arriving at the girl's father's house to negotiate betrothal and marriage. Sound familiar? Rebekah's storybook courtship with the enigmatic Isaac embodied the poetry. She was Inanna to Isaac's Dumuzi.

Rebekah was the second of four honored matriarchs of ancient Judaism: Sarah, Rebekah, Rachel, and Leah.[2] A word about the matriarchs: since the Talmud, their names have been part of the official blessing for daughters on the eve of the Sabbath. "May God make you like Sarah, Rebekah, Rachel, and Leah." Later, Midrash even credits them for saving Israel from Egypt.

> The Holy One, blessed be He, rescued Israel from Egypt only because of Sarah, Rebecca, Rachel, and Leah: as a reward for Sarah's taking hold of Hagar and bringing her to Abraham's bed; for Rebecca's saying, "I will go" when asked, "Will you go with this man?" (Gen 24:58), putting her trust in her Father in Heaven; as a reward for Rachel's taking hold of Bilhah and bringing her to Jacob's bed; as a reward for Leah's taking hold of Zilpah and bringing her to Jacob's bed. Therefore, the Holy One, blessed be He, rescued Israel from Egypt, because of the deeds of Sarah, Rebecca, Rachel, and L eah.[3]

Recently, the four matriarch's names have been parenthetically added to the Amidah, the core prayer at the heart of the Jewish worship service in some more progressive congregations.

> Praised are You, Adonai our God and God of our ancestors, God of Abraham, Isaac, and Jacob (Sarah, Rebekah, Rachel, and Leah), great, mighty, awesome, exalted God who bestows lovingkindness, Creator of all. You remember the pious deeds of our ancestors and will send a redeemer to their children's children because of Your loving nature.

So, back to Rebekah. Why is she included in this book on overlooked, misunderstood, and unappreciated women in the Old Testament? She has hardly been overlooked. Few women are more recognizable by any Christian than her. Most of us have heard about the romantic courtship and marriage to Isaac, an ancient Hallmark movie. It is the longest chapter in Genesis.

But then Isaac and Rebekah's story takes a sharp and ugly turn when she conspires to scam and defraud 132-year-old Isaac for an official blessing for her favorite son, Jacob, whose name ironically means deceiver.

For that reason, many modern Christians hesitate to honor her and the part she plays in the story of God's redemption of Israel. They argue that God agrees with them and even punishes her for her unrighteous actions. They point to two things. First, Rebekah never saw her favorite son, Jacob, again. Because of the conspiracy, his brother Esau threatened to kill him, so Jacob fled to a distant family. Second, and this is a bit obscure but very interesting. When the first matriarch, Isaac's mother, Sarah, died, she was honored by an ancient obituary.

> *And Sarah died in Kiriatharba which is Hebron in the land of Canaan; and Abraham came to eulogize Sarah and to weep over her (Genesis 23:2).*

But in Rebekah's case, the only obit is for her nurse, Deborah. Arguably, this is quite the biblical snub.

> *And Deborah, Rebekah's nurse, died, and she was buried under an oak below Bethel. So, he called its name Allon-bacuth (weeping oak) (Gen 35:8).*[4]

Is this legit? Did God punish her? Hard to say.

Many ancient Jewish scholars would strongly disagree. They have no such qualms about Rebekah. I will explain.

Here's the question. Was Rebekah a Spirit-kissed daughter of the Most High? Or was she something different altogether? What will we make of this fascinating, capable, mixed-bag, woman and distant progenitor of Jesus Himself?

Let's briefly look at her story. You can read it in Genesis 24-27.

Wealthy and eligible bachelor, Isaac, was in his forties when his mother Sarah died at the ripe old age of 127 (Gen 23:1). Abraham, who was then 137, deeply mourned the loss of his wife and buried her in a cave near Mamre. Once the mourning period was over, Abraham devised a plan to find a suitable Sarah-esque wife for his son, Isaac. Concerned that Isaac would marry a local Canaanite woman, he sent his servant, Eliezer the Damascene, to Padan-Aram, a region in Mesopotamia near where Abram separated from his father, Terah, decades before.[5] Abraham refers to Mesopotamia as "the land of my birth."

You probably know the story, but it is worth recounting. Here is Eliezer telling how he came across the beautiful Rebekah in Padam-Aram.

> *When I came to the spring today, I said, "O LORD, God of my master Abraham, if you will, please grant success to the journey on which I have come. See, I am standing beside this spring; if a*

maiden comes out to draw water and I say to her, 'Please let me
drink a little water from your jar,' and if she says to me, 'Drink,
and I'll draw water for your camels too,' let her be the one the
LORD has chosen for my master's son." (Gen 24:42-44)

No sooner had he prayed when a beautiful 15-year-old girl—who
happened to be Isaac's second cousin—joined him at the well and fulfilled
every aspect of his prayer to the last detail.

Before I finished praying in my heart, Rebekah came out, with
her jar on her shoulder. She went down to the spring and drew
water, and I said to her, "Please give me a drink." She quickly
lowered her jar from her shoulder and said, "Drink, and I'll
water your camels too." So, I drank, and she watered the camels
also. (Gen 24:45-6)

I find it interesting, and others have as well, that in their response to the
obvious miracle, both her father, Bethuel, and brother, Laban, acknowledged
Yahweh by name.

Laban and Bethuel answered, "This is from the LORD; we can
say nothing to you one way or the other" (Gen 24:50).

This led many to conclude Abraham's Mesopotamian family line had
essentially become Yahweh's followers even after 60 years had passed. Difficult
to say. We want to believe Yahwism had penetrated the extended tribe of
Abraham. We just can't be sure, and the powerful winds of other deities
regularly blew through the entire region. Monotheism was quite a rarity.

The Mesopotamians were diehard multi-theists—one earlier ancient text
lists 3600 deities. Their seven main deities included An, the god of heaven;
Enlil, the storm and wind god; Enki, the water god; Ninhursag, the goddess
of fertility and the earth; Utu, the god of justice and of the sun and his father

Nanna, god of the moon. But there were so many more, some very local, representing this or that tribe.

Is it possible, even likely, Yahweh was considered just one of a plethora of gods, maybe not even a major one in Haran? But when confronted with such a miraculous and inexplicable event, Laban and Bethuel were happy to acknowledge the God of Eliezer. Let's face it: you wouldn't want to anger the god who showed such power, would you?

Ninety or so years later, Jacob will flee to the same region. Rachel, his new bride—and cousin—will steal her father's household gods to take with her back to Israel. Hard to believe.

We really do not know Rebekah's religion or what god or goddesses she served when we first met her. I do believe she came to truly know and serve Yahweh later. The fact is Eliezer's assignment did not include the requirement that the bride only worship Yahweh. I will leave it for you to decide.

Before we get to the messy parts of the story, a few words about the birth of her twin boys. Like Sarah before her, she was barren and had to suffer with that shame for two decades before Isaac inquired of Yahweh, and she finally gave birth.[6]

Even then, she suffered from an arduous labor. Remember, this was an era when many mothers died in childbirth due to Postpartum Hemorrhage (PPH), Obstructed Labor, or Puerperal Fever. Two millennia later, in Ancient Rome, it is estimated one out of fifty mothers died in childbirth. There were no antibiotics, emergency rooms, or special care facilities. The fact she survived speaks to Rebekah's strength and fortitude. Here is the account, along with an important prophecy to her from God.

> The babies jostled each other within her, and she said, "Why is this happening to me?" So, she went to inquire of the LORD. The LORD said to her, "Two nations are in your womb, and two peoples from within you will be separated; one people will be stronger than the other, and the older will serve the younger." When the time came for her to give birth, there were twin boys in her womb. The first to come out was red, and his whole body

was like a hairy garment; so, they named him Esau. After this,
his brother came out, with his hand grasping Esau's heel; so, he
was named Jacob. Isaac was sixty years old when Rebekah gave
birth to them. (Gen 25:22-26)

The portrait of Rebekah, at least in the early years, was that of a remarkable woman. Even during her first meeting with Eliezer, she proved strong and compassionate to strangers. She easily passed the 'camel test.' I find it interesting she had a say in her betrothal (Gen 24:58). Later, Hebrew law would legislate that getting the bride's approval was unnecessary. It may have happened, but we have no actual examples. But here, in Haran, this capable woman, still a teenager, was allowed to control her future. Impressive.

I love how the Jewish Women's Archive puts it.[7] They suggest Rebekah was far more prominent than the typical woman of her day.

Rebekah is far more dynamic and proactive than Isaac, for whom no independent episode is reported. The very fact that the verb to go is used of Rebekah seven times (a number used in the Bible for emphasis) in the courtship narrative... highlights her active character. In addition, Rebekah's behavior in Genesis 24 is depicted by a series of action verbs—she runs, draws water, fills jars, and rides a camel—that contribute to a sense of her individuality and vitality in contrast to Isaac's passivity. Moreover, she is the only matriarch to receive a direct message from God... she "inquires" of God, who answers her (Gen 25:22-23)...Finally, the long courtship account of Genesis 24, which is considered by many to be a self-contained novella, can perhaps be called a woman's story. Rebekah's dynamic presence in that episode may indicate its origin in women's storytelling.

Rebekah is everything Abraham was searching for in a daughter-in-law.[8]

But then, this remarkable, almost ideal, Jewish matriarch did something that sent James Patterson-esque shock waves through the narrative. She conspired with one of her offspring to undermine her aging husband's authority.

In that culture, the first-born son, Esau, fully expected to receive the paternal blessing. Jacob (deceiver) had already tricked Esau into giving up his birthright, the lion's share of the inheritance. Jacob would now inherit Isaac's entire massive estate. Jacob was set for life. But he was not finished. Now, with the help of his mother, he set his sight on the official paternal blessing. This would make Jacob the sole heir of God's promises to Abraham and cement his position as the lone ruling power over the entire family. This was a huge deal.

It is shocking when we lay it out that way, isn't it? Jacob wants it all, even if it impoverishes his brother. Rebekah was in collusion the whole way. It seemed she orchestrated the familial coup. It reads like an episode of *Yellowstone* or *Survivor*.

Rebekah said to her son Jacob, "Look, I overheard your father say to your brother Esau, 'Bring me some game and prepare me some tasty food to eat, so that I may give you my blessing in the presence of the LORD before I die.' Now, my son, listen carefully and do what I tell you: Go out to the flock and bring me two choice young goats, so I can prepare some tasty food for your father, just the way he likes it. Then take it to your father to eat, so that he may give you his blessing before he dies." Jacob said to Rebekah his mother, "But my brother Esau is a hairy man, and I'm a man with smooth skin. What if my father touches me? I would appear to be tricking him and would bring down a curse on myself rather than a blessing." His mother said to him, "My son, let the curse fall on me. Just do what I say; go and get them for me." So, he went and got them and brought them to his mother, and she prepared some tasty food, just the way his father liked it. Then Rebekah took the best clothes of Esau her older son, which she had in the house, and put them on her younger son Jacob. She also covered his hands and the smooth part

of his neck with the goatskins. Then she handed to her son Jacob the
tasty food and the bread she had made. (Gen 27:6-17)

Granted, Isaac was virtually blind and likely pretty senile. Some suggest he
had some form of dementia. But still, this plan was extremely well thought out
and executed. Rebekah was a bold, intelligent lady who knew exactly what she
wanted and how to get it. She worked out the details. Impressive at so many
levels. But does that make it right, and is she an ideal Hebrew Jewess?

According to Jewish midrashim, the answer is "yes!" They believe Rebekah
had received a secret prophecy directly from God during her pregnancy. In their
expanded speculative storytelling, God is reported to say to Rebekah, "Esau, I
hate, and Jacob, I love."[9] So it turned out she was not a con artist but rather
a faithful servant of Yahweh doing His will. Jacob, not Esau, must become the
leader of the tribe of Abraham—no matter what. If this was true, Rebekah was
not just a matriarch of Israel but also Israel's first prophet.[10]

Some speculate Jacob wanted nothing to do with the deception. But instead,
he did it under compulsion and in shame.[11]

Confused yet? In the first Dance book, I explained one of the traits of ideal
Jewish womanhood was God-sourced wisdom and cunning.

The ideal Biblical daughters of the Most-High are somehow
also aware of the ongoing, often invisible conflict between God
and His enemies, the latter seek to destroy God's people. These
women seem willing to enter the fray no matter the cost. They
must access fantastic God-sourced wisdom, diplomacy, and
rhetorical skills to usher shalom into contentious situations—at
times without a shot fired...Daughters of the Most-High will
sometimes use disinformation, obfuscation, and even flat-out
lies in order to protect the vulnerable people of God. Today, we
have this notion that since the Ten Commandments say, "Thou
shalt not lie," that strategy is off the table. But from God's point
of view, there are times in the conflict with the enemy when
strategy calls for misinformation. It is a war, and the potential

costs are high. These ideal women with God-sourced wisdom get it. I will say more, but in war, there is a place for subterfuge.

Think of Esther when she used deception and strategy to save Israel from certain genocide. Ya'el offered hospitality to General Sisera before she drove a stake through his skull. Rahab lied to protect the Jewish spies. Midwives Shiphrah and Puah lied to Pharoah about the Jewish boy infants. Each of these women is considered a hero by the Jews, a savior, an instrument of the hands of God Himself. But each used deception to accomplish God's will.

Was this what Rebekah did? You tell me. According to Jewish scholarship, at great personal cost, Rebekah carried out God's specific will that Jacob was to be the paternal progenitor of the promised Abrahamic lineage. To accomplish the will of God, Rebekah used deceit, manipulation, and conspiracies like so many Jewish heroes, men, and women before and after her—even though it was against her husband, Isaac, the paternal head of Israel at the time. Therefore, the Jews see her as an ideal righteous woman, a hero of the faith, a model for Jewish women of all ages, and a great prophet.

Perhaps this is what Paul means when he writes,

> *And not only this, but when Rebekah also had conceived by one man, even by our father Isaac (for the children not yet being born, nor having done any good or evil, that the purpose of God according to election might stand, not of works, but of Him who calls), it was said to her, "The older shall serve the younger." As it is written, "Jacob I have loved, but Esau I have hated." Rom 9:10)*

The question for me is how to unpack the terse and enigmatic verse, "Isaac, who had a taste for wild game, loved Esau, but Rebekah loved Jacob" (Gen 25:28).

It seems we have two options: Is Rebekah righteous in her desire to have Jacob receive the blessing and fulfill God's prophecy and intent? Or was her motivation selfish due to her love for Jacob over Esau? Only God knows the hearts of men and women. What do you think?

Rebekah: The Movie

Suppose I was to direct a screenplay akin to Chosen about this family. In that case, the movie must explore the motives for Rebekah orchestrating the coup. There are reasons for Rebekah to be concerned that Esau might become the leader of the storied family.

Why the concern? Esau was a wildcard: emotional, harboring grudges, driven by his desires, with little apparent concern for others. In one scene, he rejects one of the family's traditions, arguably out of spite, and marries a couple of Canaanite women.

> When Esau was forty years old, he married Judith daughter of Beeri the Hittite, and also Basemath daughter of Elon the Hittite. They were a source of grief to Isaac and Rebekah (Gen 26:34-35).

One gets the sense of a Samson-esque-type character. Later, Esau seemed to become aware of the offense and tried to correct it, maybe some last-ditch effort to gain his father's favor again.

> Now Esau learned that Isaac had blessed Jacob and had sent him to Paddan Aram to take a wife from there, and that when he blessed him, he commanded him, "Do not marry a Canaanite woman," and that Jacob had obeyed his father and mother and had gone to Paddan Aram. Esau then realized how displeasing the Canaanite women were to his father Isaac; so, he went to Ishmael and married Mahalath, the sister of Nebaioth and daughter of Ishmael son of Abraham, in addition to the wives he already had. (Gen 28:6-9)

Perhaps Rebekah shuddered as she imagined the family with Esau at the helm—sleepless nights filled with anxiety and concern.

If I were to cast the complicated character of Esau, I would pick Israeli actor Doron Ben David. He could bring to the screen the lustiness of Esau and yet remain sympathetic. In the end, he was a tragic character.

Often, Jacob was described as a "momma's boy." That is not very helpful. If I were to guess, he had major daddy issues. He always seemed to be looking for Daddy's approval, even if he had to deceive to get it. From early on, he learned he would never be Esau, Isaac's favorite son. His subconscious struggled to fill that gap and earn some father's approval somewhere.

In the end, he would finally become "Israel" only after wrestling with daddy figures twice. The first bout was with trickster Laban over his daughters (29:16ff). The second life-clarifying cage match was with the ultimate father figure, God.

The etymology of his name gives us some thought-provoking insight. Some suggest the name Jacob (Hebrew: Ya'aqov) means "to follow" or "to be behind" but could also mean "to supplant, circumvent, assail, overreach, deceive." It can also mean "may God protect."[12]

There is one male actor who could incorporate all those concepts into a worthy portrayal of the volatile, enigmatic son of Isaac, the American Jewish actor Joaquin Phoenix.

What a film that would be with Doron Ben-David and Joaquin Phoenix on the set simultaneously. Line up the Oscars.

Who would I cast as Rebekah? British actress extraordinaire, Helen Mirren. Though not Jewish, she is tough, able to tackle complex parts and make it look so easy. She has an undying beauty and youthfulness that would serve the character of Rebekah well. In 2011, she played a Mossad agent in *The Debt*. She gives an Oscar-worthy portrayal of famous Israeli Prime Minister Golda Meir in 2023's *Golda*.

One last hire. Since this is essentially a tale about a woman, I would bring in award-winning Greta Gerwig, director of *Lady Bird* and *Little Women*, and the 2023 summer blockbuster *Barbie*. I would love to see what she would do with the memorable story of Rebekah.

Conclusion

If I am correct in my speculations, this puts Rebekah in a fascinating light. Her God-ordained quest was to utilize her natural wisdom, foresight, and capability to accomplish God's ultimate goal that the unlikely and unlikable Jacob, not Esau, would become the titular head of the family of Abraham.

Isaac had aged, perhaps had become senile, and was so enamored with Esau that he was indeed "blind." Rebekah, driven by her loyalty to the greater tribe, did what needed to be done to head off what she thought would be a disaster. Whether a specific command of God ignited it, I cannot say. Either way, this was a bold, consequential move in a culture that would condemn such an act against a patriarch. Ultimately, she appeared right about both Esau and Jacob.

What do you think? Bill@Gospel-App.com.

Let me share one more poignant insight from midrashim. They note Rebekah's birth was just before the death of Sarah in the Old Testament (Gen 22 and Gen 23, respectively). Why is this important? It seemed God ordained Sarah's successor to be born before He took her soul. "In this exposition, Sarah and Rebekah are compared to the sun that warms and spreads light throughout the world since these women illuminated the world with their righteousness."[13]

I enjoyed the provocative conclusion of the story from the Jewish Women's Archive.[14]

> Because of the centrality of Rebekah, in contrast to Isaac, the ancestral sequence might more accurately be called Abraham, Rebekah, and Jacob.

Rebekah was very special.

Now What?

I am guessing this was a very troubling chapter for some of you, maybe not how you imagined God working among His people. I get that. Suppose you are part of a group studying this book. In that case, I imagine the group is ready to explode with various responses.

I want to restore focus on one crucial aspect of the story. Ultimately, it is not about Rebekah, Isaac, or even Esau and Jacob. It is about God providentially guiding and protecting the ultimate revelation of His love for the unlovable in a lost and broken world. As always, He must use flawed people to proclaim the good news. Right?

He still does. God ordains quests for His beloved to accomplish His larger kingdom goals, often putting us in challenging, compromising, and dangerous positions. Just consider the Cross as an example. Our charge as God lovers, modern Rebekahs, is to be ready, hands-up, and eyes wide open to receive our calling—our quest.

Many people have found the Simple Uncluttered Gospel helpful to that end. Think of it as witnessing to your midbrain's critical inner voice that would bring doubt and fear even more into the equation than they already are. Say it aloud as if you were speaking to that entity. Say it twice a day for at least 45 days. Repetition is critical. There is science undergirding this prayer. We are leaning into a deeply rooted habit. Here it is. Sit back and let it wash over you.

Jesus-Follower, strictly because of what Jesus did for you 2000 years ago, Jesus loves you with all His heart, as much as the Father loves the Son and the Son loves the Father. God loves you as you are, not as you should be or could be. You can't add to this love or take away from it. It often feels like you've messed it up or need to do something so God will like you better. Not so. How do you experience it more? Simple! Ask the Spirit inside of you to make you know, experience, and feel just how much God loves you right now. Just ask. Ask again later today. Ask tomorrow. Make it a spiritual habit.[15]

What hit you? What jumped off the page? What troubled you? Rattled you? What emotions bubbled up? What word(s) offended you? Keep it up. Twice a day for 45 days. You've got this.

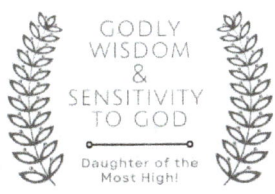

Engage Questions:

1. What did you learn that you did not know before? What difference does it make to you in your world today?

2. Who do you say Rebekah was? Was she a beautiful, capable, intelligent, and yet flawed woman who acted "problematically" in "Blessing-Gate?" Or was she a beautiful, capable, intelligent, yet flawed faithful prophet who risked all to obey God's charge to her? Or do you have other ideas?

3. If she was here today, what might she tell you?

4. On Rebekah's #8 Pillar, there would be a plague that says the Spirit gave her two powers: Godly wisdom and a sensitivity to God. Thoughts? Push back.

5. What are you experiencing through saying the Simple Uncluttered Gospel aloud to your critical inner voice? Please share if you are willing.

---

1. Klein and Sefati, Secular Love Songs, 616.

2. Ramon, Matriarchs. Some have added other 'matriarchs' including Bilhah, Zilpah and even the Beloved in the Song of Songs.

3. Kohn, Amidah.

4. Several midrashim suggest that the death of Rebekah's nurse actually referred to her own. Kadari, Rebekah.

5. Nahor (Gen 24:10) and Haran (Gen 11:31, 28:10) could be the same place or at least in the same vicinity.

6. Kadari, Rebekah. "Midrash includes Rebekah among the seven barren women who were eventually blessed with offspring: Sarah, Rebekah, Rachel, Leah, Manoah's wife, Hannah, and Zion, of whom Ps 113:9 states: "He sets the childless woman among her household as a happy mother of children."

7. Meyers, Rebekah.

8. Rebekah, Women in the Bible.

9. Likely conflating the narrative with the much later prophecy of God in Malachi, "I have loved you," says the LORD. "But you ask, 'How have you loved us?' "Was not Esau Jacob's brother?" the LORD says. "Yet I have loved Jacob." (Mal 1:2)

10. Kadari, Rebekah.

11. Kadari, Rebekah.

12. Jacob, Wikipedia.

13. Kadari, Rebekah.

14. Meyers, Rebekah.

15. You can get Women's Simple Uncluttered Gospel bookmarks at https://gospel-app.com/.

Chapter Seven

Thus Says the Lord!

"Not Doing Enough" Syndrome

What is "enoughness?" Here is David Zahl in *Seculosity*:

> Listen carefully and you'll hear [the] word "enough" everywhere, especially when it comes to the anxiety, loneliness, exhaustion, and division that plague our moment to such tragic proportions. You'll hear about people scrambling to be successful enough, happy enough, thin enough, wealthy enough, influential enough, desired enough, charitable enough, woke enough, good enough. We believe instinctively that, were we to reach some benchmark in our minds, then value, vindication, and love would be ours.

Christians pile on top of this extensive list: righteous enough, religious enough, pure enough—whatever those mean.

All of us feel the lack of enoughness at one time or another. Yet I am told that it is more common for women than men. So, here's my question. Are you feeling credible enough, respectable enough, pretty enough, lovable enough, trusted enough, believable enough, dependable enough, smart enough, discerning enough, relevant enough, spiritually gifted enough, or called enough by God? For many, the answer is tragically, "No!"

There was an insightful 2020 article in Image by Edaein OConnell, 'Not doing enough' syndrome: The female affliction of the 21st century. In it, she writes,

> It's an affliction that seems to affect every female. It's called the 'not doing enough' syndrome and we need to find the cure…" It happened while I was sitting on the Dart on my commute home. I was idly watching the world go by outside while half-listening to a podcast on how to get my ducks in order when I was hit with a realisation. One which felt like Katie Taylor had just given me a belt with her right hook. I wasn't doing enough.
>
> In work, in life, in health and in sorrow. I was severely lacking and now the cracks were showing and everyone in the world would finally see me for the farce I am. Just a week before this moment of enlightenment, I wrote a note on an affirmation tree. The note said: "You are enough." And as I sat and felt the internalised panic I had come to know as a companion, I realised how much of a hypocrite I was.
>
> It's as if women are predetermined to catch both the "I'm not doing enough" and the "I'm not good enough" syndromes. From work to home, motherhood to sisterhood, relationships to friendship–we find fault in everything we are and do.
>
> In a recent article for the Sunday Times Style magazine, writer Dolly Alderton finally put into words something I had been feeling for the majority of my life. She spoke of this impending sense of doom that she and her friends constantly feel. It's as if someone is about to pop out from behind the door and scold you for something.
>
> It's the feeling that you are about to lose your job even though

there is no reason for you to even entertain that idea. It's thinking you'll be a bad mother even though you don't plan on having children for at least 10 years. It's the feeling that this thing you call 'life' is actually an ongoing reality TV punchline, like your very own Truman Show.[1]

No judgment from me. I have struggled with enoughness insecurities all my life. At this point, feeling not enough is hardwired into my subconscious. I know in heaven, all of that will be reprogrammed. When I get there, I will scream cries of joy for weeks. For now, I take great comfort in knowing God sees me as enough strictly because of what Jesus did for me 2000 years ago. He measures me and, without hesitation, treats me as if I am just as enough as Jesus. I am enough with Jesus' enoughness. Mind-blowing, right?

One of my hopes for the Dance trilogy is that it will draw readers into the actual stories of these ancient women as they enter their quest to find enoughness in their contexts. Through the art of storytelling, we can enter their sandals as they first struggle with not-enoughness. Then, through the narrative, they come to feel a powerful, new, heaven-born enoughness in the arms of God, a little or a lot. Neuroscientist Gregory Berns notes,

> Stories shape our lives and in some cases help define a person...The neural changes that we found associated with physical sensation and movement systems suggest that reading a novel can transport you into the body of the protagonist. We already knew that good stories can put you in someone else's shoes in a figurative sense. Now we're seeing that something may also be happening biologically. [2]

The next woman, Huldah, presents an excellent opportunity to share her stunning feeling of enoughness. She was enough incarnate.

Huldah

Enter the little-known, underappreciated, and often overlooked Huldah, the prophetess. Without her, Judah's valuable societal and religious revival in the 7th century BCE would have been a confusing mess, perhaps even a non-starter. How can I say this more emphatically? Huldah provided the missing voice of God.

For her efforts, Huldah is still considered one of the seven women prophets of Israel enumerated by the Rabbis alongside Sarah, Miriam, Deborah, Hannah, Abigail, and Esther. She is also mentioned among the twenty-three truly upright and righteous women who came forth from Israel.[3]

My point, Huldah was definitely enough. She is a true hero and model for Jews and Christians of all times, but more to the point, an enough-heroine for women of all times. To quote William E. Phipps, "A woman was the first to declare Scripture holy."[4] He continued, "She began the process that culminated more than a millennium later in the canonization of the Bible."

The story of Huldah (whose name unfortunately means "weasel") began with the rise to the Judean throne of the eight-year-old Josiah in 640 BCE. He would reign as king of Judah for thirty-one years. Internationally, this was a time of relative peace in Judah because the superpower, Assyria, which had conquered the northern country of Israel eighty years earlier, was in decline and forced to worry more about local events than the distant Levant.

In only thirty-five years, at Carchemish, the rising Babylonian empire would conquer Assyria and set its sights on regional domination, including Judah. Babylon would waste little time disposing of Judah in 597 BCE, only twelve years after Josiah's death.

But our story began in 640 BCE when the boy-king Josiah came to the Judean throne. Judaism was virtually unrecognizable from earlier, better days. Josiah's father, Amon, had only reigned for a couple of years. Before that was the horrible half-century reign of his grandfather Manasseh, the fourteenth king of Judah and perhaps the most anti-Yahwistic of them all.

[Manasseh] built altars in the temple of the LORD...In both courts of the temple of the LORD, he built altars to all the starry hosts. He sacrificed his sons in the fire in the Valley of Ben Hinnom, practiced sorcery, divination and witchcraft, and consulted mediums and spiritists. He did much evil in the eyes of the LORD, provoking him to anger. He took the carved image he had made and put it in God's temple...Manasseh led Judah and the people of Jerusalem astray, so that they did more evil than the nations the LORD had destroyed before the Israelites. (2 Chr 33:4-9)

The narrator of 2 Kings also notes that the temple employed male shrine prostitutes during Manasseh's tragic reign (2 Ki 23:7).

Under Manasseh's rule, a multitude of pagan deities, primarily Baal and his consort Asherah, had replaced Yahweh. It is likely Manasseh even assassinated the great prophet, Isaiah.

Judaism virtually ceased for two generations. Judah had become a pagan nation.

But then Josiah. At age 20, Josiah began stripping the land of his grandfather's wicked aberrations.

In his twelfth year he began to purge Judah and Jerusalem of high places, Asherah poles, carved idols and cast images. Under his direction the altars of the Baals were torn down; he cut to pieces the incense altars that were above them, and smashed the Asherah poles, the idols and the images. These he broke to pieces and scattered over the graves of those who had sacrificed to them. He burned the bones of the priests on their altars, and so he purged Judah and Jerusalem. In the towns of Manasseh, Ephraim and Simeon, as far as Naphtali, and in the ruins around them, he tore down the altars and the Asherah poles and crushed the idols to powder and cut to pieces all the incense altars throughout Israel. Then he went back to Jerusalem. (2 Chr 34:3-7)

When the King turned the ripe old age of 26, he finally turned his attention to the Jerusalem Temple. He ordered the new High Priest Hilkiah to do whatever it took to return the temple to the appropriate worship of Yahweh—no small task after fifty years.[5]

Let's put ourselves in Hilkiah's sandals. For half a century, all who were loyal to Yahweh, all who knew what the worship of Yahweh looked like, had been hunted down and assassinated by Manasseh. As far as they knew, anyone and anything that had to do with Yahweh was gone and completely replaced with the religion of Baal and Asherah as the state-sponsored religion.

Here's the conundrum for Josiah and Hilkiah. There was no one left alive who knew how to run the temple. All written documents enumerating the rituals of how offerings should be handled and the day-to-day responsibilities of the priests were gone. There was no Study Bible for them to run to. What could be done?

But then, remarkably, someone found a previously undiscovered and unidentified scroll hidden in a crevice in some overlooked part of the temple. Whoever it was blew off the five decades of dust and brought it to Hilkiah. It's a great story. Humanly speaking, there are 1000 ways this could have gone sideways. If you have ever been on a worksite during a reconstruction, you know how easy it would have been for a single old scroll to get tossed out with construction debris. But some responsible priest must have looked it over and realized it might be special—a long shot, to be sure. This could be the lone remaining copy of God's written word to His people. That ignited a flurry of activity.

> *Hilkiah the priest found the Book of the Law of the LORD that had been given through Moses. Hilkiah said to Shaphan the secretary, "I have found the Book of the Law in the temple of the LORD." He gave it to Shaphan [who] informed the king, "Hilkiah the priest has given me a book." And Shaphan read from it in the presence of the king. When the king heard the words of the Law, he tore his robes. (2 Chr 34:14-20)*

Now, Hilkiah had another problem. How in the world could such a thing be validated? All the priests who might have known what this particular scroll looked like were long gone.

So, after 50 years of misuse and disrepair, Judah rebuilt the Temple of Yahweh, but no one knew what to do next. They found a scroll, but how could they discern if it was legit? Who could validate the word of the creator God? How was that to be accomplished?

Under the Old Covenant, three equal branches of authority shepherded God's people: Kings anointed to rule over them, priests who mediated between the people and God, and prophets through whom God spoke to His people.

Josiah rightly divined the scroll's validity rested under the authority of the prophets. They are the ones who speak on behalf of God. He ordered Hilkiah and his staff to find a true prophet of the Lord.

> Go and inquire of the LORD for me and for the people and for all Judah about what is written in this book that has been found. Great is the LORD's anger that burns against us because our fathers have not obeyed the words of this book; they have not acted in accordance with all that is written there concerning us. (2Ki 22:13)

I imagine Hilkiah asking, "So, does anyone know a faithful prophet of Yahweh in Jerusalem who hasn't been assassinated by Manasseh—one who still speaks the word of Yahweh to Judah? Will they come and speak to us about this scroll?"

According to rabbinic tradition, three such prophets were still active in Jerusalem when Josiah came to the throne: Jeremiah, Zephaniah, and Huldah. Jeremiah actively prophesied in the marketplaces, Zephaniah in the synagogues, and Huldah's audience consisted mainly of women at the southern gates of the temple.[6]

Why did Hilkiah send for Huldah? We can only guess. Two of the three prophets seemed to have a personal connection with the temple staff. Huldah's husband Shallum was the son of the temple official overseeing the production and maintenance of the vestments and robes of the Levites. (2 Ki 22:14). We also believe he was Jeremiah's uncle (Jer 32:7).

But for one reason or another, Hilkiah sent envoys to Huldah requesting her presence. There is no evidence they hesitated because she was a woman. Like I said, Huldah was enough.

A remarkable woman, Huldah didn't need to see or read the scroll. God had already told her directly what to say.

> *Hilkiah the priest, Ahikam, Acbor, Shaphan and Asaiah went to speak to the prophetess Huldah, who was the wife of Shallum son of Tikvah, the son of Harhas, keeper of the wardrobe. She lived in Jerusalem, in the Second District (2 Ki 22:14).*

She was in Jerusalem, living and speaking in the "Mishneh," perhaps a district near the temple. Tradition suggests that she would teach at or near the southern double gates of the temple complex. These two gates will be renamed the "Huldah" gates out of respect for her and her role in restoring the temple to its proper function.

> *She said to them, "This is what the LORD, the God of Israel, says: Tell the man who sent you to me, 'This is what the LORD says: I am going to bring disaster on this place and its people, according to everything written in the book the king of Judah has read. Because they have forsaken me and burned incense to other gods and provoked me to anger by all the idols their hands have made, my anger will burn against this place and will not be quenched.' Tell the king of Judah, who sent you to inquire of the LORD, 'This is what the LORD, the God of Israel, says concerning the words you heard: Because your heart was responsive and you humbled yourself before the LORD when you heard what I have spoken against this place and its people, that they would become accursed and laid waste, and because you tore your robes and wept in my presence, I have heard you, declares the LORD. Therefore I will*

gather you to your fathers, and you will be buried in peace. Your
eyes will not see all the disaster I am going to bring on this
place.'" So they took her answer back to the king. (2Ki 22:15-20)

Huldah needed no official audience with the King—nor wanted one. She did not need to parse line and verse of the scroll. She didn't need royal acclamation or apologies for the years the people and the rulers had ignored the prophecies from God and abused her fellow prophets. She did her job to the letter. She spoke God's word to those in power.

The discovered scroll was indeed the word of God for Judah. To his credit, Josiah unhesitatingly received the prophecy of Huldah. What Hilkiah called the "scroll of the Law" was most likely an early copy of Deuteronomy.

It brought both good and bad news to King Josiah. Bad news first, all the curses outlined in the discovered scroll would fall upon Judah. Judah's crimes against God had been extensive, and there would be a judgment. We know this took place at the hand of Babylon in 586 BCE.

Good news? Because Josiah responded to the scroll's words faithfully, he would be spared the wrath of the Babylonians.

With the scroll in hand, Josiah faithfully completed his ordained task of returning the worship of God to the land.

Josiah removed all the detestable idols from all the territory
belonging to the Israelites, and he had all who were present in
Israel serve the LORD their God. As long as he lived, they did
not fail to follow the LORD, the God of their fathers (2 Chr
34:33).

Scholars disagree on the burial place of Huldah. Many believe a grotto on the Mount of Olives holds the remains of the prophetess. Others believe that at one point in time, an actual funerary tomb structure was built over the burial site of the Jewish prophetess, just south of the two gates named after her. In either case, she is honored by Jews as a model of a righteous servant of God, male or female. Only King David's and Huldah's graves were ever allowed within the city of Jerusalem. In one midrash, Huldah rules seven sections in Paradise over the souls of pious women.[7]

Hebrew tradition suggests that there were thousands of prophets in Israel, but only prophets with prophecies containing a lesson for future generations were recorded. Rabbinical tradition has forty-eight Jewish prophets, seven Gentiles, and seven prophetesses (nebiah).[8]

The New Testament expands our list of prophetesses to include Anna (Lk 2:36-38), Philip's four daughters (1 Cor 11:5), Mary, and possibly John the Baptist's mother, Elizabeth. In Acts 2:18, Peter confirmed that the church age will be rife with both sons and daughters who prophesy (Joel 2:28).

Let me discuss Huldah's ongoing legacy in the Christian church.

The Apostolic Constitutions are an eight-book collection of early church discipline, worship, and doctrine. It has great historical significance, though questions remain about its provenance. It has been influential in parts of the Eastern Orthodox church. This prayer is recited in the ordination of deaconesses.

> Creator of man and woman, who filled Deborah, Anna, and Huldah with the Spirit...look upon our servant who is chosen for the ministry and grant your Holy Spirit.[9]

John Calvin wrote to John Knox concerning whether God would accept a woman as head of a government. He wrote,

> [T]wo years ago John Knox asked me in a private conversation what I thought about the government of women. I candidly replied...that there were occasionally women so endowed, that the singular good qualities which shone forth in them made it evident that they were raised up by divine authority; either that God designed by such examples to condemn the inactivity of men, or for the better setting forth his own glory. I brought forth Huldah and Deborah.[10]

Claudia Camp puts it succinctly,

> Modern readers, unaccustomed to thinking of ancient women
> in positions of authority, may find Huldah's story remarkable.
> The biblical evidence, however, makes clear that prophecy was a
> role open to women on an equal basis with men (other examples
> include Miriam, Deborah, and, in the New Testament, Anna),
> and the narrators of Kings and Chronicles take no notice of
> Huldah's gender.[11]

CBE (Christian Biblical Equality International) concurs,

> Huldah was a woman capable, chosen, and called of the Lord to
> be his prophetess, to be a nebiah. She was deemed competent
> of discerning divine will by King Josiah, his male royal court,
> and Hilkiah, the High Priest of Jerusalem. She was preferred by
> King Josiah above Hilkiah, the High Priest; Jeremiah, the main
> prophet of Jerusalem; Zephaniah; and Nahum to give him the
> words of God that would spur further reform and repentance
> in the kingdom and that would declare Scripture as true. One
> cannot find any disputations against Huldah's prophecies to
> King Josiah by her contemporary prophets including Jeremiah,
> Zephaniah, nor Nahum. The two passages cited, in II Kings
> and II Chronicles, clearly show that God does speak through a
> female, and that she is not under the authority of a man when
> she pronounces prophecies of the Lord.[12]

I like the charge from William Phipps, "It is time to restore Huldah to her
rightful place. She was the first to place a seal of approval on a scroll, certifying
that it contained Yahweh's genuine message. She deserves to be honored as
the patron saint of textual critics across the ages who seek to validate what is
divinely inspired."[13]

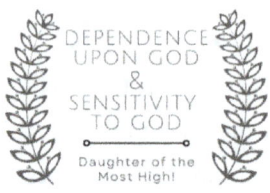

I see two ideal traits of the Daughters of the Most High clearly manifested in the life of the prophetess.

Radical Sensitivity to God and His Calling

Empowered with this fruit of the Spirit, she heard God's voice when no one else did. She knew what God wanted her to do and was empowered with a remarkable and frightening compulsion to obey, even though it could cost her life. She wasn't on her own, isolated, worried if she was "enough" in her patriarchal culture. She was confident and free to speak words to power. Whether they heard it or not was not up to her.

Dependence Upon God

Huldah was a poster child for depending upon God. This God-sourced dependence is an intentional and free reliance upon the capacity of God's Spirit alone. This is not the same as subordination or subjugation to God. Rather, it is an act of choice by an honorable free agent who understands that Godly 'righteousness' is born from dependence, not independence.

Huldah: The Movie

Who do I like for the character of Huldah? It would have to be someone who plays an intelligent and confident woman in a patriarchal setting. There must be a natural seriousness about her; still, being a servant of God, she must be able to break into cries of joy. Her character must speak truth to power without any awkwardness or apology. One person kept coming up as I searched for Jewish actresses. If she were willing and available, she would do Huldah justice. Bebe Neuwirth came to fame in the old comedy *Cheers* but since has won two prime time Emmys. She has a Tony for her work on *Sweet Charity*. Look at her bio and let me know what you think.

Huldah and Skinny Jeans

Blogger Patty Bechtold is helpful for those women who wonder if they are feeling "not-enoughness."

> Think about the roller coaster of trends in women's jeans during the past 20 years. It begins with the fashion industry, dictating new jean styles as a way to encourage women to spend more money. And then, when an influencer or a woman who is well known starts wearing the new jean style other women jump on board. One day you look up and see those jeans everywhere. You get used to them even though you may not even like them at first (I mean, skinny jeans? Whose idea was that?). Although you're probably not consciously aware of it, a subtle internal pressure to fit in moves you to adopt this style. And there is a certain kind of relief in that—moving away from not enoughness towards enoughness—even if you have to lay down on the bed to zip up your jeans. My point is that we mimic other people's choices and go along with what is expected of us because we don't necessarily feel safe being our unique, complex selves. And unfortunately that sets us up to be right back in the war of enoughness vs. not enoughness.[14]

Ladies, next time you see those skinny jeans in your closet, remember Huldah never wore skinny jeans. Empowered by the Spirit of God, she felt enough.

Be encouraged and dance, daughters of the Most High. In the eyes of God within that critically important context, at that moment in Israel's and the Church of Christ's history, clearly and unmistakably, Huldah was enough.

The next chapter will examine the very misunderstood Shulammite of the Song of Songs. It is the most extraordinary gospel presentation in the Old Testament.

Engage Questions:

1. What did you learn that you did not know before? What difference does it make to you in your world today?

2. Were you encouraged by Huldah and her story in the Bible? Explain.

3. If you can, please share any changes or spiritual "aha moments" you've noticed from saying the Simple Uncluttered Gospel every day.

---

1. OConnell, *Not Doing Enough*.

2. Clark, *Novel*.

3. Kadari, *Huldah*.

4. Phipps, *A Woman*.

5. Hilkiah is the son of Shallum who served as High Priest for much of Manasseh's tenure.

6. Kadari, *Huldah*.

7. Warren, *A Woman's Work*.

8. Warren, *A Woman's Work*.

9. Warren, *A Woman's Work*.

10. Warren, *A Woman's Work*.

11. Camp, *Huldah*.

12. Warren, *A Woman's Work*.

13. Phipps, *A Woman.* .

14. Bechtold, *Enoughness.*

Chapter Eight

Dark Yet Lovely

T he last woman in *Dance Book 2* deserves an exceptional #8 Pillar in our hallowed hall of the Daughters of the Most High. Every generation must hear her story told and retold. I believe she represents the greatest gospel presentation in the entire Old Testament.

Sadly, she is unnamed. For our purposes, we will refer to her as the Shulammite, for that is how she is referenced twice in one verse of the 117 verses of highly structured Hebrew poetry.

> *Come back, come back, O Shulammite; come back, come back, that we may gaze on you! Why would you gaze on the Shulammite as on the dance of Mahanaim? (Song 6:13).*

Scholars debate as to what the name refers to. The root of 'Shulammite' is the Hebrew word for peace and shalom, emotional and relational wholeness. Maybe she was a woman who had found identity-level wholeness. Others suggest the name alludes to her sometimes purported husband, Solomon (Hebrew: Shelomoh). Still, others see her name as an ancient poetic epithet for the city of Jerusalem (yeru-shalayim). She could be the "woman of Jerusalem."[1]

So, who was she? That has been a topic of heated discussion for a couple of millennia. Historically, many believed she was an allegorical representation of Israel or the Church, though very few hold that point of view today. In more recent history, it was popular to imagine she was the daughter of Pharoah, whom Solomon married to form an alliance of peace (1 Ki 3:1, 7:8-12) between the two countries. Others suggest she was the Shunemmite servant girl, Abishag, a young virgin chosen to keep the aging King David warm in his bed during his last days (1 Ki 1:2).

Another recent creative suggestion imagines her as the daughter of Abinadab the Gibeonite, in whose house the Ark of the Covenant resided for a time during the reign of King David (1 Sam 7:1).[2] Solomon would have been familiar with the city of Gibeon and was even given a vision from God there (1 Ki 3:4-5). If Abinadab had a daughter, Solomon might have met her and fallen in love. The Gibeonites lived just a short journey northwest of Jerusalem. They were known for their vineyards and winemaking skills and were believed by some to be dark-skinned (Song 1:5).

Most commentators today see her as a fictional generic bride to the generic king-groom. As such, they suggest the book gives us biblical insights regarding courtship and marriage.

After over a decade of scholarly research, speaking, and writing on the book, it doesn't matter who she was or if she was merely an ancient Hebrew poetic metaphor. The incalculable value of this woman to both the Christian and Jewish faiths remains off the chart.

It may be offensive to some readers who have been taught something different about the Song of Songs or her. Consider this before you make a judgment. Everyone is familiar with Jesus' famous parable of the prodigal son. Here's my question. Would the story's impact change if Jesus was speaking about an actual adolescent named "Bob?" You tell me.

Whoever or whatever she was, I would like to put her forward as a patron saint candidate for today's adolescent girls—and, for that matter, women of all ages.

Girls, she gets you.

Please take a moment and listen to her powerful self-awareness at the beginning of her story. Three Hebrew words, "Dark am I, yet lovely" (Song 1:5). This self-awareness reflects her inner struggles and her journey towards self-acceptance. I could picture her saying this to her counselor.

The Counselor's Office

"Shul, it is good to meet you. You are safe here. Everything you tell me as your counselor is confidential. So, the floor is yours. Relax and tell me what you want to talk about?"

"Well, '*Dark am I, yet lovely...dark like the tents of Kedar, like the tent curtains of Solomon. Do not stare at me because I am dark, because I am darkened by the sun. My mother's sons were angry with me and made me take care of the vineyards; my own vineyard I have neglected' (Song 1:5-6).*"

"Wow, okay, let's get right into it then. I am picking up a theme. What does it mean to you that you are 'dark?'"

"Yeah, I did say that a lot. As you know, my fiancé is the king. I love it, but I am worried it could all unravel. I mean, look at me. I am not a pampered white-skin courtier. Gorgeous, royal women, surround him. They know what to say, how to act, and which fork to use for salads. Look at me; I am from across the track, blue-collar. My family works in one of the myriads of vineyards that the king owns. You can see my dark, sunburned skin. Everybody knows. Everybody sees but him. I'm an embarrassment. I'm a field laborer, trailer trash, not a princess worthy of his love."

"I see your dilemma. Is there anything else you would like to share? You mentioned words such as being darkened, burned, and angry. What do they mean to you?"

"Life hasn't been easy for me. It's like... it's like everyone wants to hurt me, to use me, and then throw me out. There's the sun, there's my brothers...I, uh, just..."

"You are wondering if anyone would really love you? As you are?"

"Yeah, that's partly it. The king seems to, but I am not sure I am that lovable. And I am not sure I know how to love him back. Nothing has hurt me more than relationships gone bad. And they've all gone bad. I haven't been in any relationship where I really felt loved before—why start now? I am terrified of this one."

"Uh huh, and you mentioned not keeping your vineyard. I assume you are not talking about a plot of grape vines. Do you mean that you have had sex? Your 'vineyard' has not been saved for marriage?"

"Well, I am ashamed. This is in confidence, right? The truth is that I haven't been chaste. I am not a virgin."

[Note: We don't know if she lost her virginity by choice or if it was forced upon her. We don't know if it happened once or more than that. In her culture, either way, fair or unfair, she had lost personal and societal value. Inside her head, that nasty, critical inner voice kept telling her she would be found out and exposed as an unworthy bride to everyone. That would give the king another reason to drop her and find someone else—and give the daughters of Jerusalem and her brothers another reason to despise her. Deep in her soul, she feared the king would discover her dirty, hidden secret.]

"What does the king think about that?"

"Well, that's just it. I am not sure the king knows. He will find out. And when he does, this fairy tale romance will blow up in my face, and I will get burned again. I am afraid...no, I'm terrified. It is affecting me and our relationship."

"What do you mean?"

"Well, the other day, I blew up at the king. I don't know what got into me. It was like a paranoia took over. He was gone for most of the day. He didn't tell me where he was. Something inside my head knew he was cheating on me...you know, with someone more royal and more 'enough,' more lovely, less dark. I blurted out, 'Tell me, you whom I love, where you graze your flock and where you rest your sheep at midday. Why should I be like a veiled woman beside the flocks of your friends?'" (Song 1:7)

"What did you mean by that?"

"Well, you know how sex workers follow the shepherds into the fields to get business...in the field, they call it 'grazing their flocks' and 'resting your sheep.' You get it, right? I felt like I had to follow the king around like that, too. I felt like the king's whore. I was so angry."

"Has he done anything to make you think he sees you that way?"

"Oh, no, he's been wonderful and crazy loyal."

"What did he say when you accused him of betrayal?"

"Well, that made it even worse. He said,

'If you do not know, most beautiful of women, follow the tracks of the sheep and graze your young goats by the tents of the shepherds. I liken you, my darling, to a mare harnessed to one of the chariots of Pharaoh. Your cheeks are beautiful with earrings, your neck with strings of jewels. We will make you earrings of gold, studded with silver." (Song 1:8-11)

"When he said, 'follow the tracks,' what do you think he was saying?"

"I know now; he was letting me know his heart, life, and emotions are an open book to me."

"And that's bad?"

"Oh, no, that is the most amazing thing anyone has ever told me. What's the matter with me that I can't enjoy it? It's too good to believe. I can't believe it. I love him, but I am terrified it will blow up. I am afraid one day he will look at me, I mean really look at me and see that ignorant, menial, field worker. Sure, she is lovely, but she's way too dark. I worry that when he wakes up from his romance-induced stupor, he will see me as a drag on his reputation, grow tired of me, and drop me like a hot potato. I am exhausted."

Can you relate a little? Breathe it in—the emotional ambivalence of the Shulammite's feeling 'dark yet lovely,' good yet bad, attractive yet having uglies, lovable yet also unlovable, enough yet lacking enoughness, secure and insecure. Do you hear her beat-up soul? Let it resonate with yours a bit. Breathe again.

First, it is impressive self-awareness for a girl who is likely no more than 12 to 14 years old in a pre-psychiatric era. This was long before Oprah, Brené

Brown, or Taylor Swift. I imagine you have or certainly know someone who has experienced self-destructive emotions like this at one time or another, whether you are young or old. It is part of the human experience.

In her story, where we find her, and more importantly, where God finds her, she is right in front of her mirror, feeling like she will never measure up to the king's standards of being lovable enough. She is exhausted and terrified.

Remember, I said the Shulammite 'gets you.' In her article, "Teenage Girls are Facing Impossible Expectations," Rachel Simmons says,

> [Girls] tell me they are under pressure to be superhuman: ambitious, smart and hardworking, athletic, pretty and sexy, socially active, nice and popular – both online and off....The sheer impossibility of measuring up has left a generation of girls with the enduring belief that, no matter how many achievements, they are not enough as they are. The path their mothers and grandmothers cleared so their girls could enjoy every opportunity is marked by self criticism, overthinking, and fear of failure.[3]

"I've talked to thousands of girls around the country, and they tell me that they feel like their lives today are one endless performance," agrees Donna Jackson Nakazawa, author of *Girls on the Brink: Helping Our Daughters Thrive in an Era of Increased Anxiety, Depression and Social Media*. "They are performing to be liked and followed online, they are performing at school, and they are exhausted." [4]

But then God...

The Wedding

There is so much in the Song of Songs worth unpacking. I won't be able to do it justice here. I co-authored a book with Colleen Pepper called *The Kiss of God* that delves deeper into the emotional struggle the Shulammite was going through. I am currently writing another book that expands on this even more.

I want to focus on the grand marriage between the king and the Shulammite in this book.

First, let's discuss a contextual note. Our modern Western weddings are bride-centric. The bride is the focal point of the entire event.

How can you tell? The groom and his entire entourage virtually appear at the front of the venue with little fanfare, amidst what sounds a lot like elevator music. The groom has an honor guard of sorts, in full dress—which separates him in glory from the attendees a little bit—but he leads his own procession—a ceremony of lesser honor. No one stands to applaud him. In fact, he blends into the crowd with everyone waiting for someone of real value to arrive.

Also, he only wears a boutonniere, which I believe is French for the tiniest, most unimpressive flower you can find. It could be translated as microscopic or infinitesimal.

Then, the music shifts. One after another, resplendent women enter the venue, raising the audience's expectations higher and higher. Someone of great glory is about to arrive. The music becomes a great fanfare, worthy of only someone of great glory and value, and...

Enter the bride.

When she arrives at the venue's back door, all eyes are instantly on her. She is transcendent. Everything she wears was picked to that end. She doesn't merely have a boutonniere. She has a whole collage of flowers—an entire garden—a virtual ecosystem. The entire scene is directed and produced to ascribe glory to her and her position as the bride. And it works. All stand, all eyes are upon her, and everyone's breath is taken away by her majesty, splendor, and imposing beauty.

Our weddings are clearly bride-centric. Having said that, if you missed the next transaction, you missed something important. Did you notice her eyes, her gaze? If she was the lightning rod for all the glory in the room—who did she bestow glory on through her gaze?

Her eyes are adoringly upon the groom.

While the wedding ceremony is bride-centric by design, the ultimate recipient of that glory is the groom; he is the beneficiary of her gaze. By looking at him alone, she bestows him with honor and glory. The groom is raised from his boutonniere-esque ordinariness through the bride's eyes. He began as just a guy with an itty-bitty flower, but then he became the actual center of attention. Why? Because he is with her, and she adores him. The bride and the groom are both transformed through the bride-centric event.

In contrast, during ancient times, weddings were groom-centric. Here is the Shulammite's account of the wedding day.

> *Who is this coming up from the desert like a column of smoke, perfumed with myrrh and incense made from all the spices of the merchant? Look! It is Solomon's carriage, escorted by sixty warriors, the noblest of Israel, all of them wearing the sword, all experienced in battle, each with his sword at his side, prepared for the terrors of the night. King Solomon made for himself the carriage; he made it of wood from Lebanon. Its posts, he made of silver, its base of gold. Its seat was upholstered with purple, its interior lovingly inlaid by the daughters of Jerusalem. Come out, you daughters of Zion, and look at King Solomon wearing the crown, the crown with which his mother crowned him on the day of his wedding, the day his heart rejoiced. (Song 3:6-11)*

This was certainly not a budget event. This glorious affair would no doubt take the breath away of all the attendees. The focus is primarily on the king. He even wears the crown of David. "Look at him," the queen says, realizing her position in the societal food chain. She is in awe of the groom's "je ne sais quoi." Knowing the Shulammite as we do, she most likely feels some of her usual insecurities and fears. I suspect her emotions are swinging with great fluidity between dark and lovely. Wouldn't you agree? Seeing the king again in all his splendor likely wakes her critical inner voice's cackle, "See, you don't belong here. Everybody knows it. The king will know it too when he sees you."

Let's have some fun and put that ancient marriage in a modern setting! Picture blocks and blocks of the entourage coming to the church—a police escort in front and rear. Roadblocks along the way to keep wannabes out. It is a public holiday, so people are standing there, some waiting for hours to catch a glimpse of the immaculate wedding party. There are marching bands, open cars filled with dignitaries, confetti, flags waving...and then here comes the groom—in a unique black Cadillac limousine nicknamed 'the Beast' that extends for an entire block, it would seem, surrounded by secret service agents, all willing to take a bullet for him.

You are the bride waiting at the church. As you hear the sound of the king's arrival outside, your heart pounds. Your bridesmaids abandon you to go outside to welcome the king. All you hear is the roaring of approval. The cacophony of his glory comes closer and closer. The groomsmen enter one at a time, with great fanfare, each looking more stunning than the one before.

Then a silence—a pregnant pause. Trumpets blast, cries go up, all heads turn, knees bow—finally at the door—at last—it is him! All eyes are upon him—rightly so. That is where all the glory in the room rests. Are you jealous? No.

Your heart explodes at one glance of him in all his revealed glory. But what stuns you the most—what causes your knees to buckle, your face to flush—is that his full attention is directly on you! While everyone else is focused on him, he is utterly obsessed with you. At that moment, all the glory which is rightly his is now yours. He bestows it to you by his gaze.

Doesn't this hit you as a bit sexist? Well, in one sense, yes. But to say that is to miss the whole mechanism of the event. In groom-centric marriages, the glory of the event comes to the bride through the eyes of the groom—the more glory afforded to the groom, the more glory received by the bride.

Today, in the West, it is just the opposite. The more glory afforded to the bride—the more glory received by the groom. All grooms get it. We don't begrudge the bride the glory. We taste it, too, but through her eyes.

At that moment, the Shulammite's identity has been changed, transformed, rescued, and energized. Why? She is loved by the glorious one. She is held in awe of him, with him, and through him. She doesn't care at that moment that everybody is looking at him. She has felt him looking adoringly at her. For a moment, she feels not only loved, but lovable. She is enough. She is lovely. Make sense?

In our story, as they are standing together, eye to eye, hand in hand, the king whispers the most amazing thing to his bride: chapter 4, verse 1.

"Hinnak Yapha, Ra'yati. Hinnak Yapha." It is a guttural, visceral sound, hardly the stuff of great poetry.

"Look at you! Beautiful. My beloved. Look at you! Beautiful." It needs an editor for sure, but not for her. She hears it. Her soul leaps for joy at his words and the clumsiness in which his love is expressed.

The king continues.

> *All beautiful you are, my darling; there is no flaw in you...You have stolen my heart, my sister, my bride; you have stolen my heart with one glance of your eyes, with one jewel of your necklace (Song 4:7-9).*

He sees no flaw. In his eyes, in his estimation, she is not 'dark yet lovely,' she is most lovely. Then, the most surprising thing happens. The great king makes up a word. We translate it as "You have stolen my heart," but literally, he says, "You have heart-hearted me." He continues, "It only took a single glance from your eyes." He is publicly confessing the power her gaze has over him. Can you imagine how that made her feel? How would you feel?

We don't have to wait long. In Song 8:10, the bride gives us her testimony, describing the moment she finally truly experienced his love. One wonders if this was the first time she experienced love of any kind.

> *Thus I have become in his eyes like one finding wholeness (Song 8:10).*

This is so great. If you missed everything else and got this, it is worth the price of admission.

She is confessing she is no longer the same woman, "Since I became (perfect tense—I became at a certain point of time in the past and it is still true)—in his eyes (through his loving measuring gaze)—shalom."

"So, Shul, tell me in your own words what happened."

"It's hard to explain. It was as if I could finally look into his eyes. I mean, I had seen his eyes often before. But this time, it was different. For some reason, I think I saw me as he saw me—my reflection in his eyes. Does that make sense? The me that I saw in his gaze was so different from the me I saw in my brother's eyes, or the daughters of Jerusalem, or even in my mirror."

"Then what happened?"

"For the first time I can remember, I felt a wave of enoughness wash over me. For the first time, I felt loved and loveable. I became shalom."

"You mean you became your name, the Shulamite?"

"Yes, I suppose so."

Are you following? The king's love empowered her to finally look up into his vulnerable eyes and, for the first time, see who she was to him. Her reflection in his eyes overcame her reflection in all the other downward-looking eyes, her brothers, the sun, the daughters of Jerusalem, and even her own. She found and became, in that moment, shalom—the Shulammite.

Remember where the king found her? She was insecure, dark yet lovely, relationally and emotionally exhausted, a self-proclaimed failure whom nobody wanted. Nothing had hurt her more than bad relationships, and they were all bad: her former lovers (implied), her family, the other ladies, and her peers all looked down on her, and even creation burned her. No one would have voted her the "Most Likely to Succeed," much less the one to become the king's bride.

She was her own worst enemy; some might say self-destructive. She was paranoid, concerned over the king's faithfulness, worried that he would leave her for another. She even ditched his romantic advances once with something quite reminiscent: "Not tonight, I've got a headache!" (Song 5:2-3).

Even so, this wonderfully stubborn king loved her. Everyone could see it but her. He just kept pursuing her and loving her as she was. The more he pursued, the more terrified she became. No judgment; we've all been there.

How was it finally resolved? It took a power that lovers are quite familiar with, the power embedded in a true lover's gaze. That kind of love can overcome terror. The Apostle John seems to get this. There is a single perfect love that can even cast out fear. (1 John 4:18) She experienced that.

The Gospel of the Shulammite

It doesn't matter who you believe the Shulammite was. It does not matter whether she was an actual historical individual or a poetic device. Biblically, her story is a brilliant gospel presentation hidden far too long in the shadows of the Old Testament.

God has long desired and pursued His bride. Please do not hear me say that He is pursuing a worthy bride. Hardly! No one rises to that level—not by God's standards. All are dark yet lovely. The shocking thing is that He pursues an unworthy bride because He understands His unique and powerful love alone makes the unworthy bride worthy.

Here's theologian John Barclay speaking about this "incongruous gift" of Christ. He could have easily said the same thing about our worthiness as a bride.

> Paul, we shall see, had an unusual, creative, and socially radical understanding of the grace of God, arising from the Gift: Christ. Whereas good gifts were (and still are) normally thought to be distributed best to fitting or worthy recipients, Paul took the Christ-gift, the ultimate gift of God to the world, to be given without regard to worth, and in the absence of worth—an unconditioned or incongruous gift that did not match the worth of its recipients but created it.[5]

It is the love of God that makes the unlovable feel lovable, the unloved feel loved, and the dark feel lovely—the unworthy bride worthy. It is what He does.

Here is the big reveal. The Shulammite doesn't only represent women to God. God chose a woman to represent all women and men who have become the bride of Christ. Quite an honor! This is not a male or female thing. It is a redeeming gospel thing. To that largely patriarchal culture, God's best gospel presentation was quite feminine. You have to love God's sense of humor.

When God finds both women and men, we are relationally and emotionally exhausted, our identities wearied and fractured, seeking but never quite finding shalom in any venue or relationship. We feel lost. We struggle with love of any kind. We struggle with feeling unlovable and unloved.

Then God... He pursues us, finds us, and loves us as we are. The betrothal period continues until the moment we are grabbed by the power of his love. Then we hear his words to us: "Hinnak, Yapha, Rayati, Hinnak, Yapha." And we get it.

Our souls were designed for and long for this—this relationship that, subconsciously, we know is out there for us somewhere. It is a human thing. History records all of us frantically looking for it in all the wrong places until God...and we become the Shulammite.

Shulammite: The Movie

I am so excited about who I cast to play the Shulammite. Gen Z Jewish actress Marisa Abela is a great pick. She is busy, but I trust she will have her agent contact us about this part. She is known for her role in HBO's *Industry* and Sky One's *COBRA*. She even plays Amy Winehouse in the 2024 biopic *Back to Black*. I would get make-up to give her grunge, multicolored hair spikes, and cover her with henna tattoos.

Assurance of God's Favor

To this point in the book, we have seen examples of four of the five fingerprints of the Holy Spirit in the lives of these amazing women. The Shulammite manifests what it looks and feels like to experience the remarkable and unbelievable assurance of God's favor.

The Spirit empowered her to begin to grasp the limitless love of God for her as she was—dark yet lovely—not as she should be or could be (cf. Eph. 3:14-21). The love of God revealed and experienced that makes the unlovable, loveable. To be clear, God adores the dark yet lovely. That is the gift of the Gospel.

Here's Paul in Ephesians 3 talking about the very same spiritual fruit.

> *For this reason, I kneel before the Father, from whom his whole family in heaven and on earth derives its name. I pray that out of his glorious riches he may strengthen you with power through his Spirit in your inner being, so that Christ may dwell in your hearts through faith. And I pray that you, being rooted and established in love, may have power, together with all the saints, to grasp how wide and long and high and deep is the love of Christ, and to know this love that surpasses knowledge — that you may be filled to the measure of all the fullness of God. Now to him who is able to do immeasurably more than all we ask or imagine, according to his power that is at work within us, to him be glory in the church and in Christ Jesus throughout all generations, forever and ever! Amen. (Eph 3:14-21)*

The Shulammite began to experience the vastness of the love of the groom, and it changed her. Or maybe better, she finally became herself, the Shalomed-one.

As I said in the first chapter, this fruit of the Spirit is such good news for modern women and girls who feel overlooked, exhausted, and diminished by culture—those who feel a little like second-class citizens. This applies to men, to o.

God is actively inviting women and men today to dance the same dance. To be kissed over and over by the same kiss (Song 1:2).

Here's what I imagine in the great and hallowed hall of the Daughters of the Most High. I see the great hall filled with #8 Pillars after #8 Pillars, rotating concentrically around a single massive column reaching to the skies. This center column represents the #8 Pillar of the Shulammite. Why is her story central to the venue? She personifies the experience of all the other great women. Like the Shulammite, God found each of them, to one degree or another, 'dark yet lovely.' Each lady had her own story, of course. Still, none of them 'became' shalom until God's Spirit pursued and came upon them in power, bestowing ample wedding gifts such as an uncommon sensitivity to God, supernatural wisdom, righteousness, dependence upon God, and, of course, an assurance of God's love and favor.

In a real sense, the Shulammite represents them all. Equally so, she embodies all the dark yet lovely men who have been embraced and loved by God as well.

I would invite anyone who has experienced such favor from God to take a marker and write their initials on the central Shulammite column, men and women. This might strike you as vulgar and messy. I suggest that it expresses unity and intimacy.

I would love to hear what you think.

Engage Questions:

1. What did you learn that you did not know before? What difference could this make in the world today?

2. What did you feel as you heard the Shulammite's story? Explain.

3. Did you learn something new about the Gospel? Please share any spiritual "aha's."

---

1. Bloch, *Shulamite: Bible*

2. Shulamite, Biblical Research.

3. Simmons, *Teenage Girls*.

4. Cohen, *Girls*.

5. Barclay, Paul and the Power of Grace, 82.

Chapter Nine

In Closing

Y ou are probably familiar with this event in the life and ministry of Jesus. Please sit back and read it afresh. I have some closing thoughts you will find encouraging and hopeful.

A few days later, when Jesus again entered Capernaum, the people heard that he had come home. They gathered in such large numbers that there was no room left, not even outside the door, and he preached the word to them. Some men came, bringing to him a paralyzed man, carried by four of them. Since they could not get him to Jesus because of the crowd, they made an opening in the roof above Jesus by digging through it and then lowered the mat the man was lying on. When Jesus saw their faith, he said to the paralyzed man, "Son, your sins are forgiven." Now some teachers of the law were sitting there, thinking to themselves, "Why does this fellow talk like that? He's blaspheming! Who can forgive sins but God alone?" Immediately Jesus knew in his spirit that this was what they were thinking in their hearts, and he said to them, "Why are you thinking these things? Which is easier: to say to this paralyzed man, 'Your sins are forgiven,' or to say, 'Get up, take

your mat and walk'? But I want you to know that the Son of Man
has authority on earth to forgive sins." So he said to the man, "I tell
you, get up, take your mat and go home." He got up, took his mat
and walked out in full view of them all. This amazed everyone
and they praised God, saying, "We have never seen anything like
this!" (Mark 2:2-12)

Remember the story? Did something new jump off the page as you read it? Here's what struck me as I thought more deeply about the account. I understand there was no mention of women, though undoubtedly many were there.

This exhibits the powerful reflection of the heart of God—not sedentary, not sitting on a distant throne looking through creation to find someone worthy or loveable He can use for His agenda. I see a moving, energetic, rescuing, caring, and healing God.

Here are my thoughts. If the four friends of the paralyzed man hadn't climbed up on the roof and lowered their friend in front of Jesus for healing, God Himself would have blown the roof off the hut and lowered the man down to the care of His Son. God loved that man so much and desired that he get up and walk, nothing would have stopped Him. There is no evidence the man was particularly righteous, good, or worthy. But at that moment, he became a case-in-point, illustrating to all of us the love of God for broken, unworthy, helpless people—men and women equally.

This is what God does. He finds the exhausted, overlooked, misunderstood, and underappreciated people—men and women—and with love, he pursues them, fills them with his Spirit, and raises them up for their next ordained quest of honor. Arguably, their compromised situations were, in fact, the beginnings of their Pillar-earning quests.

The stories in this volume mirror the workings of such a God in the lives of regular women. God didn't find Himself in a bind, unable to locate a man to step up and so shrugged His Holy shoulders and said, "Well, I guess I have to do the task with a woman." Not at all. These women may or may not have been honored by their culture, but God always honored them.

It is not that God finally noticed these women. No, that would be absurd. It is far better to believe He intentionally chose them to receive the quest designed for them before time began. Of course, they had a choice whether or not to accept their quest. But empowered by the Spirit's fruit, what else would they choose?

I have written a series of award-winning fantasies for 10 to 15-year-old young readers inspired by C.S. Lewis's Chronicles of Narnia—a shameless plug, to be sure.

The Kingdom Quests series takes place in a kingdom ruled by a great king who is not what he appears to be. There are quirky dragons, gnomes, trolls, spiders, and, of course, giants. The stories are littered with great quests, spirit caves, injustices, and many troubles and challenges.

In the third book in the Kingdom Quest trilogy, *The Garden Tale*, the kingdom of the great king is at war, and the once-flourishing Garden City seems lost. A mysterious evil character, Dolos, has duped the inhabitants into believing no king exists. It is a brilliant strategy. And that's not all. Dolos has flooded the streets with a dangerous drug that has all the residents of Garden City addicted and under his control. The king sends a hand-picked task force to save Garden City, but by the time they arrive, there appears to be little, if anything, that can be done. The need is too overwhelming.

One of the king's task force members is a very capable counselor, Anelé. As she gazes at the vast sea of devastated men, women, boys, and girls of Garden City, each under the control of dark forces, she quickly feels unqualified and starts to question herself. Painful memories of her past make matters worse. In her home country, 'coloureds' like her were considered almost subhuman. Women coloureds even more so. "Who do you think you are," said her critical inner voice, "to think you could make a difference here? Why would the king even think of sending you, of all people?"

Let me share an extended excerpt from the book that many will relate to, particularly those of you who have not felt equipped or worthy of your quest.

"I think...," Anelé says, sharing her deep fears with the very Scottish Royal Vizier, Nomos.

"I think what's bothering me the most is that it's my story all over again, man."

Anelé leaned further back in her chair and massaged her tall, thin neck, hoping to relieve some of the tension. She went on.

"My parents—for a myriad of reasons that I will never understand, weren't there for me—not that way. Dad gone, my mallie (mum) so needy herself. Add to that how others treated we coloureds in general. I remember on a smelly white bus in my mallie's lap, and a large dirty blonde-haired brute stood next to us and called me a little 'hotnot.' It doesn't really mean anything. It's just a nasty made-up label like stupid, dumb animal, human refuse, or something unnecessary. Hotnots just take up space like a garbage can would. I didn't know what it was, but the way he growled it chilled me to the bone. I was so small and so vulnerable. In the end, my little-girl-enoughness-cup never got filled. Not my fault ye see. So, when I was older, I had to fill it myself with anything I could: leftovers, rubbish, drugs, cheap pick-up lines, abusive relationships that promised acceptance, where I was told I was beautiful, but I just ended up being used—again and again."

"I came to my end in a very nasty dangerous prison, so certain that I was ugly, fat, dumb, and a total loser—a hotnot. Shame, yeah? There was no rescuer—not for unlovable coloured women like me. I deserved the gang. It was my punishment, yes."

"Nomos, it's the same with the people that I spoke with in here. Dolos has won, bru. They are broken."

It was time for the Royal Vizier Nomos to say his piece. He paused, nodding his head as he gathered his thoughts. He slowly reached his stubby hand into his colorful vest and pulled out his Scottish long pipe and placed it elegantly between his lips. It was a beautiful long bent pipe, clearly made by a skilled craftsman, no doubt in his home hills around Edinburgh. Nomos says that its equal is not to be found anywhere. It sports a beautiful natural dark brown finish, yet the long wood veins are clearly noticeable. I should add that Nomos no longer smokes. He gave it up years ago, it's a horrible habit. But he still enjoys 'wearing it' he calls it. He is a sight to behold.

"With all due respect, yer bums oot the windae? (Scottish for 'You are not thinking straight!') I told you earlier, Dolos is just another blockhead, an eejit (idiot), or a boggin lavvy head (foul-smelling toilet head). He is definitely a liar and very powerful, but he is hardly creative and certainly not as powerful as the great King."

"Are you saying that the King is still here?" Anelé said with a gasp, breaking into Nomos' story. "...That he reigns over this blight?"

"Hmmm, has anyone ever told ya...This great King is just not what he appears. He's the ruler over many kingdoms, more than we can imagine. So, nothing would be more likely."

Anelé took a deep, cleansing breath. The stress lines on her forehead disappeared. What Nomos said seemed to bring some solace to her.

"Nomos, I need to know. What is this place? Is it the Kingdom? Is it a trick of Dolos? Is it drug induced?"

"That is not the right question, dearie. Better, what is the purpose behind all of this, and even behind the evil of Dolos... There is something else at work. I can put it no plainer than to say that we were meant to be here in this place at this time, in this celestial battle with Dolos in the name of the great King and on behalf of these very needy people. And that's an encouraging thought. Even though the very wise cannot see all ends, my heart tells me that Dolos [has] a part to play yet, before the end. He would be wildly upset to hear me say that, but so it is."

"So why me?" asked Anele in frustration and self-doubt. "Why am I here, and not someone more qualified? I did not ask for this. I am ill-prepared."

"Such a question cannot be answered...But you and I have been chosen for this quest and you and I have chosen to go. Yes? So, isn't it reasonable then that no matter what, we should use all of the strength, wisdom, and compassion that we have? I believe that all will end according to the ultimate design. These chance meetings (Nomos used air quotes) are not mere fortune, fate, or toss of the dice. As truly as this is their quest," Nomos waved his arms over at the gathered people, "this is also our quest, ordained by the great King himself. Even so, the specific purpose is not clear to me,"

"So, I could have refused this quest?"

"Aye, of course, we are no' slaves here. What good king would have forced an empty-cup hotnot to do what she wouldn't do?" Anelé chuckled.

Nomos went on. "But you see, you did accept. Whenever we take on something for one reason, but something other than what we hoped for happened instead, we ignorantly call it chance, or fate, or a miracle, but that so-called chance occurred because of a mysterious order which ultimately flows from the throne. It disposes all things ultimately for good—even things unknown to us, unseen by us. It brings the events together—to their high end. Such order and purpose, cause and effect always exists at a level far above our sight and awareness, and largely due to our innate ignorance and lack of creativity, the result, the eucatastrophic (good) end of the tale, the inevitable consolation may seem like mere happenstance. But King help us, no. All happenings in the kingdom exist and move mysteriously under the watchful eye of the benevolent providence of our great King. Freedom of choice and the fates appear to we earthbound dependent on each other. So, it is and so it must be."

Nomos paused and realized that he had been pontificating.

"Oh dear," his puffy cheeks turning red. "It must be the Yorkshire tea; I fear I have said too much."

"Let me say one last thing," he continued, "and then we have work to do. Maybe it will help. Our lives are made up of many quests from the hand of the King. Some we ask for. Others, he gives us unaware. This is who this King is. So, to be sure, this 'other' kingdom is also on its own quest. We are here as messengers of the King, to remind the needy here that the King still loves the unlovable, the unloved, and the unlovely—even hotnots—no matter how far they've veered off their own quest—no matter how they resist that love."

"All I do know is that this manifestation of the Kingdom is no' separate from the King and the King's embrace. Those people in there may no' remember the King, aye, but he remembers them and whatever craziness and lies have got them all jumbled up, have no power against the King."

"Like you say, girl, they're emptied cups that need fillin'. Like you, like me, they need to hear of the real King, the one who is and who exists even here—even though he is no' now seen. The good word is that the great King still loves the unlovable addicts too, not because they are worthy, or good, or even loyal. No, it is his love that gives them worth."

"Do no' misunderstand. There are no doubt a few here who truly hate the king and will never follow, never receive. They are adamantly aligned with Dolos and his lot and will suffer his fate when the time comes. Nevertheless, the King can and will still use them for his ultimately good purposes. That he will."

"I believe most here are just made blind by Dolos' silly parlor tricks. The King will make them see again."

"We are privileged to be a part of his rescue. Do not think all too highly of yourself. We are not the rescuers, never, we only point to the only one who truly loves the unloved."

The stories in *Dance Daughters of the Most High!* are more about God than these women. It is more about His love for them, as they were, than their love for Him. The stories are more about God calling these women to enter great quests beyond their experience and capability which ultimately afford them a new name and greater honor. This is what God did then for these incredible women and still does for women today.

Abigail, the unfortunate wife of the fool Nabal, was an unexpected hero. Her quest, written, produced, and directed by God, elevated her to heroic status, a true mother of Israel. She was the surprising person, raised up by God at that time, and at that place to prevent David from doing something that, humanly speaking, could have torpedoed his future as king.

Who could have imagined two lowly Hebrew midwives would somehow save the nation of Israel? This is beyond anything Tolkien, Lewis, or J.K Rowling would have created. Who would have been less prepared and equipped to challenge the leader of the greatest nation in the world at that time? But God saw it differently. He saw them differently. Their quest was to save the people of God. They did it. They almost single-handedly prevented a genocide of the Jewish race. What a story. What a spectacular quest.

Tamar, not even a Jew, accepted her God-given quest to hold fast to what she believed was the heavenly-ordained lineage of Abrahamic promises—though she risked her name, reputation, and even her life.

When God needed someone to care for the physical needs of his prophet, he commanded a Gentile widow to step up. Certainly, others were more qualified or had more food or more strength. But that was not the story God was writing. He chose her. Her quest was to believe a deity she had never heard of would make such a thing happen.

Huldah was raised up as a prophet after a long season of great anti-Yahwistic oppression so that once God raised up a new faithful king, she would be there and ready to authenticate his holy scroll as true. Couldn't God have called up one of the more famous male prophets? Wouldn't they have been more prestigious and credible? No. This is the story God wrote.

The matriarch Rebekah's charge was to protect the God-ordained line of blessing even though it required her to conspire against her husband. Can you imagine?

The Shulammite's quest was to finally, against every fiber of her being, look into the eyes of the king and be loved. This is often the most difficult of all quests for us. I can't imagine anyone less prepared to do that. And yet, she is the one God called and empowered to that end. For all eternity, she is the main character of the God-parable that proclaims His love for the unlovable, the unloved, and the unlovely. Anyone, male or female, can now read the account and believe that if God could romance her, He could romance even me—even you.

One of our deepest hopes is that through sharing the stories of these daughters of the Most High, we have torpedoed any notion that God can only use the smart, the fit, the super-talented, this or that sex, or socio-economic category, family or nation of origin, the religious, or even the powerful. It matters little to him whether you are male or female, overlooked, dismissed, how you've been treated up to this point, or whether you have screwed up your life big time. Your culture, family, society, or tribe may have dismissed you for some reason. None of those things will hinder God from calling you to your ordained quest—one that might change the world. None of those things will prevent you from achieving the glory and honor God has in store for you. This Great King is just not what He appears.

One last time, I want to invite you to repeat this gospel presentation designed for you, beloved Daughters of the Most High. I invite you to say it aloud to your nasty, critical inner voice at least twice daily.

Jesus-Follower, daughter of the Most-High, strictly because of what Jesus did for you 2000 years ago, Jesus loves you with all His heart, as much as the Father loves the Son and the Son loves the Father. God loves you as you are, not as you should be or could be. You can't add to this love or take away from it. It often feels like you've messed it up or need to do something so God will like you better. Not so. How do you experience it more? Simple! Ask the Spirit inside of you to make you know, experience, and feel just how much God loves you right now. Just ask. Ask again later today. Ask tomorrow. Make it a spiritual habit.

Then dance, Daughter of the Most-High, dance (Eph 3:14-21).[1]

Take note of what words jumped off the page for you. That could be telling. What made you cry? What troubled you? Perhaps they offer some new clues for the quest you are on.

In the next *Dance Daughters of the Most High! Book 3*, we will look at some overlooked, misunderstood, and unappreciated women of the New Testament. I can't wait to hear what you think.

In closing, it seems appropriate to use the Shulammite's own words. I suggest we put these words on a massive plaque over the door to the great hall of #8 Pillars of the Daughters of the Most High. This is what humans feel once grabbed and embraced by God. The quest is over; mighty things have been accomplished in His name, so the women and men rejoice and sing of the King.

> *Let him kiss me with the kisses of his mouth—for your love is more delightful than wine. Pleasing is the fragrance of your perfumes; your name is like perfume poured out. No wonder the maidens love you! Take me away with you—let us hurry! Let the king bring me into his chambers. We rejoice and delight in you; we will praise your love more than wine. How right they are to adore you! (Song 1:2-4)*

Whew! Welcome to the dance, Daughters of the Most High!

Engage Questions:

1. What did you learn that you did not know before? What difference does it make to you in your world today?

2. What is your God-ordained quest? It is likely something you feel unqualified to accomplish. That would be God's sense of humor, wouldn't it? What might your #8 Pillar say?

3. Many are troubled with the notion that God has written, produced, and directed great quests for all of us. Please share your thoughts.

4. This presentation of the Shulammite might differ from what you have previously heard. Push back. You are a person of great honor here.

5. What struck you when you heard the Simple Uncluttered Gospel this time? Was there a single word or phrase that jumped off the page? Did something bother you? Do you agree with the SUG? Please share any thoughts.

---

1. You can get Women's Simple Uncluttered Gospel bookmarks at https://gospel-app.

Chapter Ten

Also By Dr. Bill Senyard

Fresh Inspirational Women's Devotional

Dance is a fresh and timely look at seven of the most often overlooked, underappreciated, and misunderstood women in the Old Testament, written for individual and small group studies.

- Did you know there was a woman who almost single-handedly saved the line of Jesus? Her story reads like a Mission Impossible thriller.
- One woman snatched her city from a rampaging general, keeping David's fragile kingdom from splintering further.

"Dance is a powerful piece of writing that will motivate readers to reanalyze the role of the neglected women of biblical times. This book will become one of the prime selections in the canon of religious literature." Z. Sheikh, Reader's Favorite Reviewer.

Insightful and Transforming Biblical Historic Fiction

These are the long-lost journals of the Apostle Matthew. He and a colorful team of men and women followed the dangerous missionary charge of Jesus to go into all the world—in their case, Ethiopia—and preach the Gospel. Matthew's team was a striking testimony to the saving grace of their Lord. There was a former prostitute, a recovering opium addict, a shamed African princess, a freed Roman slave, and even a former member of the Sanhedrin who was present that evening Jesus was condemned to die.

"The Rabboni is a captivating journey through history, offering a compelling blend of biblical scholarship and storytelling that will resonate very well with readers interested in the early Christian era." Award Winning Author, K.C. Finn

Exciting and Fun Fantasy for Young and Old Readers

Inspired by C.S. Lewis' Chronicles of Narnia. 18-year-old 'unlikely' Prince Yeled wanted to finally prove to his adoptive father that he was worthy of being the prince heir. But what could he possibly do? He asks for a quest—no, a great quest—no, a heroically astonishing quest—challenging enough to prove his enoughness and finally earn the King's respect and love. Yeled will learn through thrilling, quirky, and sometimes unbelievable twists and turns that not all quests are what they might seem, and more importantly, this King is definitely not what he appears.

"Chronicles meets Princess Bride."

"Life Changing" Fantasy For Young Readers and Adults!

The Storyteller's Tale is the second book in the Kingdom Quest Trilogy, combining thrilling adventure, epic fantasy, unforgettable characters, witty humor, and life-changing lessons for young tweens and teens.

Cutthroat pirates kidnap the renowned royal storyteller, Berenice, but the abduction raises perplexing questions. It appears hidden forces in the kingdom are determined to expose her long-kept, dark secrets. What—or who—is driving this dangerous game? At what cost? Is it revenge? Punishment? Or something even more frightening?

Remember, not all quests are alike...and this King is definitely not what he appears.

Third Book in the Kingdom Quest Trilogy

The Garden Tale combines thrilling coming-of-age adventure, epic fantasy, unforgettable characters, witty humor and relevant life-changing lessons for today's young readers. A specially selected royal team embarks on a dangerous mission. Garden City is under siege by a fierce enemy, sparking a great war. The conflict is not between armies of knights, trolls, dragons and dwarves, but something far more devastating and destructive. Can the kingdom survive this onslaught? The answer lies in the pages of The Garden Tale. Remember, not all quests are alike...and this King is definitely not what he appears.

Praise for Other Award-Winning Kingdom Quest trilogy books:
"Sometimes, it's the most profound truths communicated so simply that make a real difference." -Library Thing Reviewer

"Senyard crafts a unique premise with a fresh and fascinating moral puzzle at its center. Fast, funny, fantasy of trolls, dwarves, a missing king, and social media." -BookLife Review

Chapter Eleven

Bibliography

- Barclay, John, *Paul and the Power of Grace*, Grand Rapids: Eerdmans, 2020.

- Barmash, Pamela, "Tamar's Extraordinary Risk: A Narrative—not a Law—of Yibbum," The Torah.com, 2016. .

- Bechtold, Patty, "Enoughness vs. Not Enoughness: Let's Call a Truce", Wise Life Therapy & Coaching. August 26, 2023.

- Bloch, Chana. "Shulammite: Bible." *Shalvi/Hyman Encyclopedia of Jewish Women*. 20 March 2009. Jewish Women's Archive.

- Budin, Stephanie, *The Myth of Sacred Prostitution in Antiquity*. New York: Cambridge University Press, 2008

- Bull, Michael, "The Toledoth as Decalogue," Bible Matrix, April, 2020, https://www.biblematrix.com.au/the-toledoth-as-decalogue/

- Camp, Claudia, "Huldah: Bible" Shalvi/Hyman Encyclopedia of Jewish Women. December 31, 1999. Jewish Women's Archive. .

- Cherry, Kendra, "Signs of Low Emotional Intelligence," VeryWell Mind, November 8, 2022. .

- Clark, Carol, "A Novel Looks at How Stories May Change The Brain." Emory University eScience Commons. December 17, 2013.

- Cohen, Sandy, "Girls are struggling with their mental health. Here's what parents can do," UCLA Health, Apr 3, 2024,

- Fisher, Eugene J.. "Cultic Prostitution in the Ancient Near East? A Reassessment." Biblical Theology Bulletin 6 (1976): 225 - 236.

- Frymer-Kensky, Tikva. "Tamar: Bible." Shalvi/Hyman Encyclopedia of Jewish Women. June 23, 2021. Jewish Women's Archive.

- Herodotus, *Herodotus*, The Histories, A. D. Godley, Ed. Hdt. 1.199.

- *Hospitality*, Jewish Virtual Library, .

- *Jacob*, Wikipedia, Wikimedia Foundation, May 24, 2024, https://en.wikipedia.org/wiki/Jacob_(name)

- Kadari, Tamar. "Abigail: Midrash and Aggadah." Shalvi/Hyman Encyclopedia of Jewish Women. December 31, 1999. Jewish Women's Archive. .

- ———, "Huldah the Prophet: Midrash and Aggadah." Shalvi/Hyman Encyclopedia of Jewish Women. December 31, 1999. Jewish Women's Archive.

- ———, "Rebekah: Midrash and Aggadah." Shalvi/Hyman Encyclopedia of Jewish Women. December 31, 1999. Jewish Women's Archive. .

- ———, "Shua's daughter: Midrash and Aggadah." Shalvi/Hyman Encyclopedia of Jewish Women. December 31, 1999. Jewish Women's Archive. .

- ———, "Tamar: Midrash and Aggadah." Shalvi/Hyman Encyclopedia of Jewish Women. December 31, 1999. Jewish Women's Archive.

- ———, "Widow of Zarephath: Midrash and Aggadah." Shalvi/Hyman Encyclopedia of Jewish Women. December 31, 1999. Jewish Women's Archive. .

- Klein, Jacob, Sefati, Yitschak: *"Secular" Love Songs in Mesopotamian Literature*. In: Cohen, Chaim/et al [Ed.]: Birkat Shalom. Studies in the Bible, Ancient Near Eastern Literature, and Postbiblical Judaism Presented to Shalom M. Paul on the Occasion of His Seventieth Birthday

- Kohn, Daniel, "The Amidah," My Jewish Learning, https://www.myjewishlearning.com/article/the-amidah/.

- Maller, Allen, "Amazing Jewish women: Abigail." The Times of Israel, July 8, 2014.

- Meyers, Carol, "Rebekah: Bible." Shalvi/Hyman Encyclopedia of Jewish Women. June 23, 2021. Jewish Women's Archive. .

- Moore, Chandler, Brown, Chris, Raine, Naomi, and Furtick, Steven, "Jireh", Old Church Basement, Elevation Worship & Maverick City, 2 021. .

- OConnell, Edaein, "Not doing enough' syndrome: The female affliction of the 21st century." Image, Jan 20, 2020. .

- Phipps, William, "A Woman Was the First to Declare Scripture Holy." Bible Review 6 (April 1990): 14-15, 44.

- Ramon, Einat. " Matriarchs: A Liturgical and Theological Category." Shalvi/Hyman Encyclopedia of Jewish Women. December 31, 1999. Jewish Women's Archive.

- *Rebekah*,   Women   in   the   Bible, https://womeninscripture.com/rebekah/.

- *Shiphrah and Puah*, Wikipedia, Wikimedia Foundation, Feb 16, 2024,

- *Shulamite*,   Biblical   Research,   Jan   30,   2018. https://garispire.com/geography/2018/1/30/shulamite.

- Simmons, Rachel, "Teenage Girls are Facing Impossible Expectations," CNN Opinion,

- Stol, Marten. *Women in the Ancient Near East,* Berlin, Boston: De Gruyter, 2016.

- Warren, Brenda Griffin, "A Woman's Work: How God used Huldah to change the heart of a king and a nation." Priscilla Papers, Spring 2003, Vol 17, No. 2.

- Zahl, David. *Seculosity: How Career, Parenting, Technology, Food, Politics, and Romance Became Our New Religion and What to Do about It*, David Zahl, Broadleaf Books, 2020. 109-126.

www.ingramcontent.com/pod-product-compliance
Lightning Source LLC
Chambersburg PA
CBHW070751120626
46557CB00002B/540